Annie Turner has been training dogs and has studied pack-animal and hunting instincts for many years. Her dedication helped her understand the way animals think not only in the wild but also their inbuilt instincts, enabling her to bring out the dogs' natural ability to train and be obedient at all times. She has become well known as the animal whisperer. Due to her unique methods and understanding, she was sometimes referred to as Dr Dogology. All this set the road ahead for the future and what she loved best—dogs and their natural pack-animal instincts and their way of thinking—which remains today.

To my wonderful husband, Steve, a huge thank you for being by my side all the way through in finishing this book.

Annie Turner

WHISPERING DOGS

From the Beginning, Basic Training Made Easy

AUSTIN MACAULEY PUBLISHERS™

LONDON • CAMBRIDGE • NEW YORK • SHARJAH

A CIP catalogue record for this title is available from the British Library.

ISBN 9781528946810 (Paperback)
ISBN 9781528946827 (Hardback)
ISBN 9781528971966 (ePub e-book)

www.austinmacauley.com

First Published (2021)
Austin Macauley Publishers Ltd
25 Canada Square
Canary Wharf
London
E14 5LQ

A big thank you to Austin Macauley in helping me publish this book. To Roddy and Norma McKenzie for pictures of Sky. To Dean Claxton for the lovely pictures of his puppy, Jessy. To the Pact Animal Sanctuary for the work they do and the pictures they have provided. Many thanks to Colin Vogel for pictures of Ginny. To Justin from Sunny Side Vets in Kings Lynn for all his advice, help and photos. To Tom Ryves of Norfolk Trading Ltd in Swaffham, letting me take endless photos of his supplies and products, again a big thank you. To Richard Wilkins for his kind help, advice, support and pointing me in the right direction, and as he would say, "Oh, what the heck!" I would like to thank every man and his dog.

Contents

Chapter 1

From the Beginning

Whether your chosen puppy is going to be either a working dog or a pet, a puppy is not difficult to train. It takes a lot of time and patience and an open mind and the ability to think forward outside the box. If you always have this in mind, you won't go wrong. The longer it takes in training a youngster the better the outcome for the pup in learning. Never shout at a pup but always keep a gentle tone. Some pups are softer natured than others, whereas other pups are more boisterous. I find that a quieter type of person may find a softer-natured pup much easier to train. Likewise, a more outgoing person may consider a bolder type of pup easier to train.

Choosing a Puppy

What's best, bitch or dog?

Once you have chosen the breed of puppy, you want the one that will best suit you. You will then have to consider whether you want a bitch or a dog. This is sometimes the hardest decision because the one puppy that catches your eye might be a dog when you want a bitch or vice versa. I have had many people come and pick from a litter and say, "that one is nice, but I wanted the opposite sex" or "I must have a black and white pup" or "it's got to be a bitch." The colour does not make any difference to how the puppy will turn out. What I would say, though, is that whatever you pick, you have to like what you are looking at, but the most important thing is the sex of the puppy not the colour of it.

You may also need to consider when choosing a bitch that the bitch will come into season twice a year. If you are not going to have her neutered, you will have to make sure your garden is well fenced in order not just to keep her in but also keep unwanted dogs out too. Like both sexes, all dogs have an incredible sense of smell, especially when a bitch is on heat. I have known unwanted male dogs clamber up and over a 5-foot fence to get to a bitch on heat. I have also experienced even the smaller terrier type males squeeze through the smallest gap between a fence to get to the bitch. The last thing you want is someone else's dog to get to your bitch, so just bare this in mind and make sure you have adequate fencing that is high enough to stop even the largest of dogs climbing over the fence, and, likewise, make sure there are no gaps between the fences either.

If you have no intention of breeding from the bitch, the other solution will be to have the bitch neutered. This stops all the bother of the bitch having a heat every six months and also unwanted visitors sniffing around. While I am on the subject of choosing a bitch, training will have to be halted while the bitch is on heat as her system and thoughts will be on overdrive. She will show very little interest, and besides this, her focus will be on elsewhere: male dogs. You can count at least six weeks of every six months where the bitch will be out of action. Also, if you don't have her neutered, she could run the possibility of developing phantom pregnancies. This, in itself, can be from slight to a serious condition. Firstly, she will start to nurse items; her nipples will start to swell depending on how serious the phantom pregnancy is. A few years ago, I actually saw the bitch's neck and head swell. This bitch, in particular, was so full of milk, it travelled up to her neck. This may never happen but beware, it could.

Some bitches will get snappy because they are feeling broody. If the bitch does produce milk, you will have to keep an eye on her. She will constantly lick her nipples, and doing this will increase the milk flow, which then could develop into mastitis. At this point, my aim is not to put anyone off having a bitch, but if you're not planning on breeding from her, you would be wiser to consider having her neutered. This will then take all the problems out the way of her having six-monthly heats and any other associated problems that may come with it. It will also keep away the unwanted male dog visitors as well.

You may also have to think about your choice if you already have another dog at home. This may be a male dog and you may like another of the same sex, or you already have a bitch and want another bitch as a companion. It may be your first puppy as a replacement of an older dog you have recently lost. I prefer bitches, that is my preference, but I have also had male dogs over the years. I do not believe the old wives' tale that bitches are better than male dogs and are easier to train. It's all down to the owner: how you are with the puppy, how you handle it, the time given and plenty of patience. All puppies have their own different characters just like human beings. Some are soft-natured and some are more of a boisterous nature. No two puppies are ever alike. This will have to be taken into consideration especially when training the youngster. You will also need to keep in mind your needs and personality and the nature of the pup.

There are several factors to consider when choosing a male or a bitch puppy. Unneutered male dogs are much more territorial than bitches. This is true but when a bitch is in heat, she can become very territorial. Male dogs especially will want to leave their scent mark, by peeing up trees, walls, lamp posts, anything they can find when out and about in an attempt to leave their scent mark on everything they possibly can find, which is a natural reaction; even when in the wild, they would do just that. Male dogs are more likely to display a greater urge to guard and patrol the home and the territory it lives in, guarding the family against unwanted strangers, and will be more aggressive towards other strange dogs or strange people than a bitch would be. Whereas an unneutered dog will also display certain types of unwanted behaviour towards other strange bitches, particularly if she is in heat, to attract them to mate.

Another thing to take into consideration when choosing the sex of a puppy is that unneutered male dogs will often have the desire to roam and are more likely to wander off when you are out walking, in an attempt to escape from the garden looking for a bitch in heat. A male dog will almost do anything to find a bitch in heat so he can mate with and leave his mark, this is a strong pack animal instinct which they still have today. Whereas, unneutered bitches do not tend to roam as male dogs do. However, when a bitch is in heat, their characters and moods may change, and they may wander to try and find a male dog to mate with. Whatever the sex you choose, prevention is better than cure, so make sure your garden is well fenced and secure.

Unneutered male dogs and bitches will be driven with a strong urge, as they would in the wild as a pack animal, to mate and reproduce offspring. Male dogs are different as they have a much more stronger urge than bitches, and a bitch will only have this urge when she is in heat. Male dogs will be more dominant, outgoing and territorial than a bitch and sometimes become more aggressive towards other male dogs, which is again to be the dominant leader of the pack. This means that male dogs may roam more in search of a mate, as outlined above, and generally be more dominant, outgoing and territorial than bitches or neutered male dogs. They may also show very odd sexual behaviour at times, trying to mount different objects, i.e., furniture, toys or even someone's leg, especially when they get over-excited. They generally, at times, appear to have a one-track mind and will do this to another dog within the family, because this is inbuilt in them. Even two neutered bitches that live together in the same home will display this sort of behaviour from time to time. Two unneutered male dogs are much more likely to show signs of aggression towards one other, and this behaviour will escalate if two dogs are in competition against one another—when a bitch is in heat—to mate and leave their mark to produce offspring and also to be the pack leader. This is what they would do in the wild. In a situation like this, if two male dogs become aggressive and fight, potentially, the outcome will be extremely vicious towards one another because of the fight for dominance and to produce offspring. This is so very strong in them. You must remember that dogs today are domesticated, underneath all of this they still have the wolf pack animal instinct in them, which remains today in all dogs.

An unneutered bitch will often go through something of a personality change when they are in heat and can become extremely clingy, wanting more than normal affection or human contact. On the other hand, they may become withdrawn and very shy. A bitch may also actively look for a male dog to mate with and show odd behaviour at times wanting to go out more by sitting at the door or not wanting to remain in the garden or not wanting to come into the house. If you have another dog, she may try to mount the other dog in an attempt to try and stimulate her desire to mate and breed, which is natural. Unneutered bitches tend to be more tolerant of other unneutered bitch. If you are thinking of buying two bitch puppies, in order for them to keep one another company and have a playmate, you must remember that two bitches that are in heat together can show signs of aggression towards one another and become territorial. Having two bitches together, one being in heat can also bring the other bitch in heat at the same time and, again, they can show aggression and strange behaviour towards one another as this is pure dominance between the two of them.

Usually, a male or a bitch, neutered or unneutered, will often build a strong, lasting lifetime bond with their owners and neither a male or a bitch will be any different in terms of which is more loyal to their owners. This will generally come down to how you train and handle the dog's lifestyle, also how you interact with it from the start and through the dog's life.

Handling the New Puppy
The Correct Way to Pick Up a Puppy

The correct way to pick up a puppy: the puppy should be supported with both hands under its front and back legs to avoid pressure being placed on its internal organs.

1. **Place your hand under the puppy's chest**: Use your hand to support the puppy's chest, where the rib cage is. You'll need to go in from the side of the puppy, placing your hand either between the puppy's front legs or around under the front legs.
2. **Support the puppy's back end**: As you lift the puppy up, use your other hand to support under or between the puppy's back legs and bottom.
3. **Lifting the puppy up**: Once your hands are in position, slowly and gently lift the puppy up. Make sure you continue to support both the puppy's chest, back legs and bottom as you hold it. You can pull the puppy close to your body to give it extra support, if needed. Remember, the puppy may wriggle. Do not hold the puppy away from you as the puppy may wriggle out of your arms and injure himself by twisting.
4. **Place the puppy down in the same way**: When putting the puppy back on the floor, make sure you are still supporting the puppy's chest and back legs and bottom. Gently lower the puppy onto the floor.
5. **Most importantly, never grab the puppy by its head, neck, legs or tail.** You could injure the puppy or even kill it.

Never pick up a youngster under its front legs, leaving its back legs hanging unsupported. The result of this, later on, could cause back problems. Picking a puppy up like this makes their back muscles contract and twist to one side. More so as well, picking a puppy up from under its front underarms puts great pressure on its internal organs and rib cage, again causing problems later on that could go unnoticed as the youngster grows, which, in turn, could have serious consequences.

Chapter 2

The Healthy Puppy

If you buy a pedigree puppy, always buy from a well-known established breeder. Never buy a puppy that is advertised on a roadside or a puppy from an accidental mating. Even in some of the top pedigrees, inherent defects can miss several generations and come out somewhat twenty years later or so. This is why it is important to look carefully at the Kennel Club Pedigree and make sure both sides of the pedigree are not too closely related to one another, most importantly from the point of view that a good bloodline on both sides means a better quality puppy, and also if you are considering breeding at a later date, or if you are choosing the puppy for a working dog, the bloodline in a working dog will be very important as well. The pedigree should and will indicate field trial champions and winners within the pedigree.

If possible, ask for a copy of the original Kennel Club Pedigree before you see the litter so you can do some research on what you are possibly considering to buy. The reason why I ask to see the original Kennel Club Pedigree is that anyone can put together the most fantastic pedigree with field trial winners and champions going back generations. So, it's very important to see the original Kennel Club Pedigree. This will give you time to do a little research on what you are buying. Observe the mother and if possible, the father of the puppies as well. Taking this into consideration, the mother after having a litter may not be at her best as the puppies will have taken the energy out of her. But overall, it will give you an idea of any inherent problems she may or may not have. Both the mother and father of the puppies should be sound in body and health. If either of the parents show any signs of defects, you should not purchase a puppy from the breeder, as this can be passed on potentially to future generations and, also, if you are considering breeding from it at a later date. Look at where you are buying the puppy from and the surroundings they live in. This will also give you a good idea about the care the breeder has given to their upbringing.

Do not buy a puppy that is housed in filthy conditions. Also take note if any of the puppies appear to have pop or bloated bellies since this will indicate they could be full of worms. Make sure the pups have been wormed on a regular basis and also the mother. Ask what food they are being fed on, how many times a day they are fed as well. Look at the mother's teeth to make sure they sit correctly and are not under or overshot. Also, look at how the mother and father stand. They should stand square. Also look for any signs of stiffness in them. Look at the pup's eyelids to make sure there is no swelling and nothing unusual and there is no inflammation or discharge. This is important as this type of condition can be passed onto puppies through generations. If the puppy comes from good solid breeding, there should be no inherent defects. Some inherent eye defects may not usually be noticeable until the pup starts to grow. At around six months of age when the head starts to mature, these inherent problems will begin to appear, causing problems with running eyes and infection.

Normal puppy head with no defects

Inherit Defects

It is always a good idea to look at each individual puppy, not just the one that catches your eye. Make sure you look at the puppy's teeth, their teeth should sit together and be pearl white in colour. If you find any of the puppy's teeth with either an overshot or undershot jaw, you do not want to pick a puppy with this condition or a puppy with any eye condition. If you want to breed, later this can be an inherent problem that can be passed on to future generations.

Normal teeth

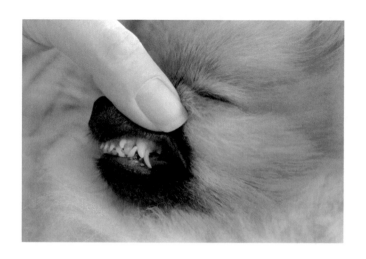

Overshot teeth

You will need to look at the puppy's umbilical button to make sure there are no lumps. This is because most bitches lay down when giving birth, but occasionally, a bitch may take longer than expected to deliver. She may stand up during this process. When the puppy comes out, it will hang, which causes a strain on the umbilical cord. The bitch will then nibble the cord to release the puppy. When the bitch is standing up to deliver the puppy, it hangs from the umbilical cord in its own sack. This may cause a small hernia around the belly button. This is another cause of small hernias, and it is quite often the case. When the bitch nibbles (severs) the umbilical cord to release the puppy from it, the bitch will sometimes nibble too close to the skin of the puppy when it is born, and hence this may cause a hernia.

Certainly, if you potentially want to breed later on and dependent on how big the hernia is, this would not be a good puppy to choose or if you seriously want the puppy as a working gundog later, this could cause problems later in life.

Vaccinations

When buying a puppy from around twelve weeks of age, it will need to be vaccinated; usually, the first vaccination will take place between eight to ten weeks of age with the second jab at around three months. There must be at least two weeks between each jab, and the puppy must be at least three months old before it receives its second jab.

It's important that all puppies are vaccinated against major canine diseases of Leptospira, Parvovirus, Canine Distemper, Para Influenza Virus and Adenovirus. Just a word of warning here. If you are considering a working gundog breed and eventually working it in the field, it's extremely important to have the pup vaccinated against Leptospira, as female brown rats carry this disease, and wherever a gundog is working, it can be transmitted to the working dog when hunting the ground, or even if you are walking your dog in woodland, it can be transmitted. Once your puppy has been jabbed, it should not have any contact whatsoever with any strange dogs or be exercised where other dogs have been for at least two weeks after receiving the vaccination. Once all the vaccinations have been done, then your veterinary surgeon will advise that your puppy will need a yearly booster vaccination for life. Over the years, there have been questions on the side effects that vaccinations have on dogs, but this is purely down to you either to have your puppy vaccinated or not, and you may want to talk with your veterinary surgeon about the side effects. I personally would rather have peace of mind knowing that the puppy will be free from disease and it has been stopped from spreading. Like all vaccinations and medication, they all have some sort of side effects, as with human being's medication has some sort of side effects. If you plan a holiday, you will have to keep this in mind because you may need to put your dog into boarding kennels and all good boarding kennels will require your dog to have up to date vaccinations.

Worms

There are two types of worms which are most commonly found in dogs and puppies: Roundworm Toxocara Canis and Tapeworm Dipylidium Caninum.

Roundworms are very common in puppies. They are long, spaghetti-like parasites that live in the puppy's gut. They can be several inches long and are white or a pinkish colour with a roundish body. They look similar to a very small earthworm. The eggs are passed out into the environment via the puppy's stools and can also be transmitted just by the puppy licking their coat. Once swallowed, the eggs get into the puppy's system. Sometimes in heavy infestation, this can lead to the larvae being released in the gut which then may travel into the lungs. The puppy or dog will cough and swallow again resulting in the larvae ending up in the stomach, and once in the stomach, the larvae will produce eggs which repeats the cycle. This can happen again and again. The worms you see in the puppy's stools are actually adult worms. If the puppy's stools are not removed straight away, some pups will eat their own stools or even other dogs' may eat other puppy stools, and the cycle then repeats itself all over again.

Tapeworms are slightly different and can be recognised by a creamy whitish colour and have a flat appearance, like long flat ribbons. They are made up of small segments. They cannot be passed from dog to dog, unlike the roundworm. Tapeworms are transmitted through fleas and ticks that have been on an infected dog, which they have fed on, and because of this, the dog may have tapeworm inside their stomach. How the cycle works: the flea will jump on a dog. The dog then licks its coat and the flea along with the eggs inside, will be swallowed by the dog. The eggs hatch and the larvae attaches itself to the intestines and, at this stage, will start to mature. Once the larvae has matured, it sheds segments containing lots of tiny eggs and is released from the worm and passed out via the puppy's stools, where they remain for some time. They look like very tiny crawling grains of rice—tiny maggots is probably the best description. Fleas are the big cause for tapeworm. If the puppy is infected with tapeworm, it is because it has accidentally swallowed a flea when licking its fur or biting its hair. It's a vicious circle, that's why if a puppy has fleas, it should be treated for worms as well in order to stop or prevent recurring infestation again and again.

If young puppy is not wormed on a regular basis, this can lead to all sort of problems. It can cause undernourished puppies with blown bellies, sometimes referred to as pop bellied. Some symptoms occur such as diarrhoea, vomiting and also coughing. This is due to the fact that the larvae has entered the lungs of the pup. It's a vicious circle and the only way to try and prevent this happening is to routinely worm on a regular basis. This will help to control the worms that are inside the dog, and the eggs and larvae that are constantly going through the dog's system.

Young dogs and puppies also need to be wormed on a regular basis as the mother will pass the roundworm larvae to her puppies. Therefore, she should also be wormed before the birth and after the birth as well. You must always ask the question before buying a puppy from the breeder whether the mother has been wormed and have the puppies been wormed as well. Asking as many questions as possible highlights the fact of the care that has been put into breeding a good, sound, healthy litter of puppies that the breeder has bred.

Puppies should be wormed at two weeks of age and every two weeks thereafter, up to twelve weeks of age. After that, they should be wormed every month up to six months until their immune system gets stronger and then every three months. The wormer should be a good quality wormer purchased from a veterinary surgeon. You can also purchase wormers from large pet stores where they will give you advice before making the purchase. Make sure you ask your veterinary first. Some stores will have in-house veterinary centres as well. There are many wormers on the market but one of the best wormers is Drontal Puppy Wormer. This is excellent for roundworm. Many puppies are born with roundworms and if not wormed, can have a critical effect on the pup's health and growth which will also lower the puppy's immune system. There is no worm treatment on the market that will give a lifetime lasting effect in controlling any type of worms, purely because the worming treatment you use will only kill off the worms that are in the adult dog or puppy's gut at the time no matter how old the dog is. This is why all puppies and adult dogs needs to be regularly treated for worms to try and prevent the worms from recurring. I would say, at this point, before making the purchase of a puppy, ask the breeder if the bitch is wormed, and also the puppies. If the breeder has not wormed the bitch or the puppies, then I would most definitely not consider buying a puppy from the breeder, I would look elsewhere.

Fleas

Typically, a female flea can lay up to 50 eggs per day. One flea can trigger an infestation in any puppy or dog. Once the flea lays its eggs in the fur of the puppy, some eggs will fall off onto the surrounding area, which could include the carpet, upholstery and the bedding your puppy lays or sleeps on. The eggs will turn into larvae, which then pupate and could lay dormant for up to six months, or even longer, re-emerging to infest its next passing host. Only five per cent of a flea infestation will be present as an adult flea on your puppy or dog. The other ninety-five per cent will be living around the house and in the bedding the puppy or dog sleeps on. This is why it's so important to flea treat not just your puppy or dog but every pet in the home, as well as spraying all your carpets at home on a regular basis with a household flea spray. This will help eradicate outbreaks of fleas recurring again and again especially in hot weather conditions. Flea spray can either be purchased at your local veterinary surgeon or can be purchased at most well-known pet stores.

All the puppies and their mother should be treated for fleas, lice and ticks, as all of these are passed on from birth by the mother. Regular treatment should be done at intervals normally on a monthly basis. Frontline, these days, can be purchased at most pet superstores, or through your veterinary surgeon. When taking your puppy to your veterinary surgeon, your veterinary can ask the veterinary nurse to complete a puppy health check on your puppy and give advice if needed. Many veterinary nurses today working in a veterinary practice will offer free health checks, so it's worthwhile going to them. It's a good idea on a weekly basis to inspect the pup for signs of flea's lice or ticks yourself. One of the tell-tale signs of an infestation is when the pup starts to scratch and bite its skin.

Inspecting the skin in some longer-haired breeds, it may be a bit more difficult in spotting the debris a flea leaves behind, which is reddish black gritty deposits in the dog's coat. This is made up of dried blood that the flea has produced after it has bitten and fed off the dog.

Signs of fleas

One of the best ways in spotting fleas is sitting the puppy or dog on a piece of white paper and then comb the dog's coat. You will find that there will be debris in the comb, or you will see small blackish-red specs, which are made up of dried blood on the paper. In an older dog, sometimes the flea debris can be so bad, the skin of the dog will look a reddish colour instead of the usual cream colour. I have also seen a dog that was so badly infected by fleas when it was bathed, the water turned red in colour. This was purely down to a severe infestation of biting fleas on the dog's skin.

All puppies and dogs should be groomed on a regular basis to try and avoid infestation of these parasites. There are many different types of shampoos and treatment on the market, but you should always follow the guidelines. I personally would seek advice from a veterinary surgeon. At the same time, the nurse will do a health check and can advise accordingly on the best available treatments for flea's lice and ticks. There are many products now that treat all three in one. Frontline today seems to be a best-seller but there also are tablets available which can be purchased on prescription that gives a three months dose against everything, including worms.

Ticks

Ticks can sometimes go unobserved on your dog. They usually go unnoticed until they mature into an adult. They sometimes resemble a small spider with an egg-shaped body, and this is why they go unnoticed. They have eight legs and may vary in size from about 1 mm to 1 cm long. They attach themselves to a host and gauge themselves on their blood. Ticks not only live on puppies and dogs but can live on any animal.

Ticks

Ticks are found more in woodland and forestry, grassland, and heath areas including riverbanks and can also be found in your garden if you live in an area with lots of surrounding woodland. The most likely places to find ticks are areas where there are deer or sheep. Ticks are active all year round, but you are more likely to see them between spring and autumn.

Ticks are different to fleas. They don't jump or fly. They can climb or drop onto your dog's coat when the dog brushes past an area the tick is sitting in. One of the places the ticks prefer to attach themselves are around the dog's neck, ears or feet because these are the places where there is less hair. Ticks can also be found between the back legs of a puppy or dog. After a walk, make sure you always brush your dog because brushing helps to remove the ticks. If you find a tick, never try and squeeze the tick or pull it off the skin of your dog. This increases the risk of infection. You can buy from any good pet store tick removal devices, which will make removing the tick a lot easier. Don't be tempted to twist or pull the tick with a pair of tweezers. Again, this can cause infection.

Ticks feed by biting an animal and having a meal on the dog's blood. This can take several days, and as they feed, they start to grow in size and mature. They will then drop off, lay their eggs and the cycle starts all over again. Ticks can also transmit microbes that can cause diseases such as Lyme disease. If you live in an area which is well-known for ticks, it's a good idea to use a regular tick treatment that will either repel ticks or kill ticks once they attach themselves to your dog as well. So prevention of fleas and ticks is better than cure. There are many spot-on treatments, tablets and collars that are available from most pet stores. You can also consult your local veterinary surgeon about which one is most suitable for your pet and the dosage required. Your veterinary surgeon may suggest an alternative treatment. If ticks persist, using the same treatment for any length of time may make the dog immune to the treatment. If you buy from a pet store, make sure you read the instructions very carefully as some treatments are for adult dogs only and not puppies, therefore the dosage will be different. As with ticks, these can be passed on from pet to humans, but it is more likely that ticks can attach themselves to humans when walking in long grass, woodlands etc. When walking your pet, make sure you wear long trousers and long sleeve clothing. This will help reduce the risk of the ticks attaching themselves to your skin.

Lyme Disease

If a dog is diagnosed with Lyme disease, the bacterial infection can be very serious and can even kill a dog or leave long-lasting health problems. Firstly, the dog may become depressed with the loss of appetite. Other symptoms may also include lameness, raised and swollen lymph glands, swollen and painful joints. The dog may run a high fever temperature. Humans can also catch Lyme disease from ticks as well, as with dogs' ticks they can also attach themselves to your skin again, this is because ticks are so small, they can go unnoticed. The symptoms can be missed for many months until the person becomes unwell. The disease can be serious, even life-threatening. If you walk your dog in any areas where they have sheep or deer, woodland or forestry, make sure you take precautions to avoid being bitten by ticks, wear long-sleeved clothing and make sure you wear long trousers.

Ear Problems

Regular inspection of the pup's ears should be done on a weekly basis which is simple to do. The youngster will soon get accustomed to this routine. In regular inspection if the ears look dirty and are a brownish black in colour, looking greasy and containing small particles of grit, there is more chance of a possible infection. This is the first sign of waste being left behind from ear mites. If you see any of these signs, treatment should be sought immediately from your local veterinary surgeon. If it is left for any length of time, this will become a breeding ground and can be passed on from dog to dog and also puppies. The irritation will also cause head shaking, excessive scratching and finally, if untreated may cause a second infection or related problems such as ear canker or haematomas. There are many products that can be purchased from most pet shops as well.

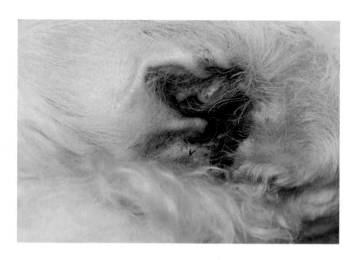

Infected ear with debris of wax and grit

Tagging (Microchipped)

It is now a compulsory requirement all puppies of eight weeks of age have to be tagged (microchipped) and this can be done through your Veterinary Nurse. Some large pet stores now have a walk-in Veterinary centre and the procedure can be done in store. If a puppy or dog gets lost at some point, it is helpful in tracing back to the owner if found. If you are considering buying a puppy and it is over eight weeks of age, ask the question has it been tagged or microchipped? If the answer is no, then don't buy the puppy, as this is now compulsory. All breeders should have all puppies tagged before they are sold to a new owner. If the breeder hasn't had the puppies tagged, they should be reported to the relevant organisation.

Just by doing a little bit of homework, while looking at a litter of puppies, will help you make your mind up whether you want to buy from the breeder or not. It also gives you the indication if the breeder is breeding good, sound quality puppies, not just trying to make some extra money. Puppies should never be sold under eight weeks of age. If the litter is registered with the Kennel Club, there are rules of when a puppy can leave its mother. So, don't be persuaded into buying a puppy under eight weeks of age. I personally like to keep my puppies until twelve weeks of age. They are well weaned and have got over the initial stress of being separated from their mother and siblings.

Assessing the Litter

Assessing the litter, once you are satisfied the puppies have been bred well, and looked after with tender, loving care, you can now consider buying a puppy from the breeder. Before you make your final choice, ask if you can see all the puppies play and interact outside with one another. This will help you again make your final choice. Don't be tempted to have two puppies just because they will keep each other company. Yes, in my opinion, they will keep each other company, but you will have twice as much work cut out for you with them. It may seem simple to have two puppies, but unless you are experienced and you know what is involved, I would advise sticking to having just one puppy. My theory is and has always been **where there is one, there is always two, and where there's two, there's trouble.** Remember, if you do take two, **they are never loyal to you, only to one another.**

The Perfect Puppy
Your Final Choice

After breeding and training dogs for many years, having two puppies together is always a handful. It may seem easy, but it is definitely not, so don't be tempted to have two puppies, thinking they will keep one another company. You will need to see all the puppies running around, this will enable you to see a bit more of their characters in general. It will also help you decide which one catches your eye. Pick up the puppy you like gently, have a good look at it, then put the puppy back with the litter, kneel down to the puppies level, clap your hands and call them, they should all come running. Now again at this point, one will shine out and take your fancy. If you think this is the one for you, ask the breeder to hold it while you pick each individual puppy up one by one. This will help make your mind up which one you want. Again, after doing this, put the puppy back with its brothers and sisters, kneel down to their level, clap your hands again and call them. The puppy should again catch your eye. At this point, this puppy will be the one for you.

You have now made up your mind which puppy you want. I would recommend if the puppy is old enough to leave the litter and its mother, you do not take it home at this point. The reason being, you will need to prepare where you are going to have the puppy for the first month or so, whether it be outside in a heated kennel or in the home. This will give you time to make sure you get prepared in advance before you bring the puppy home, especially if it's your first puppy.

Ask the breeder if you can leave a small blanket with the litter while you go home and prepare for the puppy's homecoming. You may say why leave a blanket? The reason being when you collect the puppy, you are taking it from its safe place, away from its brothers, sisters and mother for the very first time. This will be a traumatic experience for it, in surroundings that are unfamiliar, with new smells as well. Taking a blanket with the litter's smell on it will help settle the puppy in its new surroundings to some degree over the next few weeks. So, this is very important in trying to reduce the initial stress the puppy will go through. Just a small blanket will be suffice. It does not have to be a single bed size, just big enough for the blanket to be folded in half for the pup to nestle into and keep warm.

The Best Start in Life – Feeding the Puppy

Food and what a puppy is fed on is the most important part of the puppy's health, for life, growth and the puppy's bones. Make sure you ask the breeder what food the puppies are fed on and how many times a day they are fed. In my opinion, this is the best start in life for the puppies, and they should be fed on the very best with a high protein level. If they are fed on cheap food, then I would not buy a puppy. The cheaper foods may be OK for an older dog, but for digestion, the cheaper foods contain less meat and are made up more of cereal. Quite often this will have the effect of not being digested properly, quickly passing through the puppy's intestines, causing it to have diarrhoea. This is what you don't want. Using a good, high-quality meat level, preferably an all-in-one dry food that is high in protein, produced especially keeping puppies in mind. Bringing a puppy up can be very expensive. Good quality puppy food with a high level of protein can cost you around £50 or so per 15kg bag.

Puppy food can be extremely expensive, but the best must be given to the puppy in the early days if you want strong and healthy growth. When you purchase a puppy, a good breeder should provide you with a few days' supply of food which will give you time to purchase the exact food the pup has been fed initially on. Or the breeder may have a bag of food you can purchase from them. If the breeder doesn't give you any food when you take the puppy home, then I would not buy the puppy from the breeder. So, you need to ask the breeder if they will be providing a few days of food while you source the same food elsewhere.

Another question you need to ask is, how many times a day are the puppies fed? They should be fed at eight weeks of age at least four times a day. If they are only fed twice a day, I would not buy from the breeder as this could have an impact on the puppy's long-term growth. By the time they are twelve weeks, they should be on three meals a day. If a breeder is breeding good, sound quality puppies, all these little things show how much thought, care, love and attention that has gone into breeding a healthy litter.

Feeding Bowls

It's important at this stage to consider what type of bowls you will use to feed the pup. There are lots of bowls on the market. There are plastic bowls with rubber grips on the bottom to stop the bowl from sliding on the floor. There are also stainless-steel bowls.

There are also a good selection of Ceramic bowls as well. Either way, the choice is up to you but you may have to consider which ones you prefer. From my experience, firstly the plastic bowls with grips underneath seem OK for the initial few months and I say again, just for the first few months, purely because the bowls are light in weight and they don't slide across the floor when the pup is eating. The downside to the bowls being light, when the pup gets older, is that the bowls can be picked up off the floor, thrown around and also be chewed. Use of ceramic bowls is suggested as they are heavy and are more difficult to pick off the floor, and they don't slide around the floor either.

I have only found the bigger breed of dogs pick up ceramic bowls, which has ended up in them smashing them. On the other hand, stainless steel bowls do not break but the downside is, the pup that likes to play with their bowls can pick them up and clatter them on the floor, thus making the pup do this more and more.

Hard wearing ceramic bowls

Now if you have a puppy that is kennelled outside, you may consider a ceramic bowl for feeding and a ceramic bowl for water as well. Keep a spare set just in case of accidents. If you are keeping a pup inside the house, I would consider a ceramic bowl just for water so it can't be tipped up, and a stainless-steel bowl for feeding. After feeding, the stainless-steel bowl can be removed. There are also now on the market travel bowls which are fully collapsible. They are light in weight; however, they are chewable but are ideal if you're travelling your puppy a long distance where you can stop at intervals offering your puppy a drink. Or if you're taking him out in the vehicle for a walk to his favourite place, he can have a drink before going home.

Travel bowl

Chapter 3

The Journey Home

The journey home will be the first stressful time the puppy will encounter. It has been taken away from its mother and the litter. The puppy will feel frightened, insecure and alone for the very first time. Make sure you plan your journey home, especially if you have to travel a long way, and remember, don't hurry to get home. Make sure you liaise with the breeder before collecting the puppy and plan to pick up the puppy early in the morning, so the pup has plenty of time that day to settle down in its new home and surroundings. The day before, ask the breeder if the puppy could be given a light breakfast at least two hours prior to the journey home and have time to run around and relieve itself before travelling. You should be given a vaccination certificate, microchip certificate and Kennel Club Pedigree transfer documents signed by the breeder and worming records as well. The breeder will also give you instructions on how many times a day and how much the puppy is being fed. At this point, the breeder should have given you a few days' supply of puppy food, which will give you time to purchase the same food when you arrive home.

Make sure the cage in the back of your vehicle has plenty of newspaper and the original blanket you left earlier with the breeder.

At this point, I would slip around the puppy's neck a small, lightweight-material collar, calmly talk to the puppy, gently pick the puppy up and slowly place it in the cage in the back of the vehicle. Make sure you don't take too long in leaving the breeder. Take a steady ride home and try and make the journey as easy and as comfortable as possible. Your new puppy will more than likely cry, howl its socks off, whimper and also may be sick. This is purely down to stress with being in the vehicle. The blanket will help to comfort the puppy while travelling. It will have the smell of its brothers and sisters on it and will also comfort it for the next few weeks until it adjusts to its new surroundings.

If you haven't got a cage for the back of the vehicle, there are other dog transportation products on the market such as plastic car crates which come in various sizes. The crates are extremely light and compact and can be transported on the backseat of the car.

Plastic Travel Crate

Alternatively, if you don't want to use a cage or a crate and are planning taking someone to help with the puppy, you will have to make sure you take an old towel and some kitchen roll just in case the puppy is sick on its travel. Ask your helper to sit in the front passenger seat, gently pick up the puppy, wrap the original blanket around it and put the puppy in the arms of your helper. This will help the puppy feel more secure and safe. Ask your helper to speak to the puppy in a gentle tone to try and sooth it. You want to make the experience as pleasurable as possible so the puppy will experience comfortable car rides in the future. The puppy at this stage may start to whimper, or cry but this is totally normal so don't be alarmed if this happens. Your helper needs to reassure the puppy with a calm voice. Don't reinforce the puppy's fear by becoming overly excited or overly affectionate; this will only make matters worse.

A Place to Stay Inside the House

For the first few weeks, the puppy will need a place to stay inside the house somewhere secure and safe. You may want to house the pup in a large cage in the kitchen or a specific room where it can see you and hear you. Puppies tend to sleep a lot and will need their space. The cage initially will be used for sleeping and eating. The puppy will get used to having its own territory.

Make sure the cage is placed somewhere relatively quiet for the first few days. It may be worthwhile having the cage in the corner of a room near a door, preferably the kitchen door, which will help in toilet training. The cage will be the puppy's safety zone, somewhere it will feel safe and secure. I would also purchase a child's safety gate so the puppy cannot escape outside when it is loose in the kitchen. The first few days will be traumatic for the puppy; at night, it will cry a lot, even howl. My advice would be, do not keep going to it, you will only make it cry more. It will soon settle down.

The cage should have plenty of paper at one end; the other end will be its sleeping and eating area. Put the puppy in the cage on its blanket so it can settle down and sleep. Don't be alarmed if the puppy starts to whimper, cry and howl a lot; this again is normal. To help distract the pup, you may want to drape a large cloth completely over the cage, which will help settle the puppy, and eventually it will sleep. Make sure you situate the cage where the puppy is not isolated and shut away from the family, this is important. If the pup has to be confined alone for periods of time, then leave the radio on low. Metal cages come in various sizes and can either have just one opening door or two and can be purchased from most good pet suppliers.

Different cages

Alternative cages

Instead of using a cage, you may consider housing the puppy in a metal pen. One of the advantages of using a metal pen is that the puppy is contained but also can have the freedom to play and move about freely because of the extra space. The pen can also be easily folded flat and can be packed away when not in use. They come in various shapes and sizes and will accommodate the larger breeds as well. It also has the added extra that the puppy can have as bed area, feeding area and toilet area along with having a play area as well.

Different types of metal pens

Another advantage is that the pen can also be used outside in good weather. There are a number of pens you can purchase on the market, and again depending on the size your puppy will grow to, you can purchase larger pens as well.

What Bedding to Use

There are several different types of bedding on the market, you can also buy online as well. But keep in mind once the pup starts chewing, this may include its bed as well. You also need to consider the puppy will need toilet training. I find the best bedding to use is shredded paper. The soiled bits can be removed easily, and by using shredded paper, the pup won't usually want to eat the bedding. The bedding can be fluffed up on a daily basis so the young pup can snuggle into it to sleep. I still use shredded paper bedding on all my puppies and also on adult dogs as well. Straw bedding can be used but sometimes straw will harbour ticks which are transferred to the pup and even older dogs. If you do use straw bedding, make sure it's from a well-known supplier. Most pet shops and equestrian shops stock straw in bales and can be readily acquired at very reasonable prices. Also, the straw is well aired and has not been kept in damp conditions. Shredded paper is particularly good in a cage where the pup will spend a lot of its time sleeping.

Other good types of puppy and dog beds you can buy are made of soft material. These can be just flat duvet types, circular soft material beds that vary in size as the pup grows These types of beds are okay initially but can be chewed at a later date when the puppy starts to shed its teeth.

Soft bed

You can nowadays buy indestructible beds. They are made of very hard canvas-type material and are often sold as indestructible, but beware, these can be very expensive and I have not found, as yet, any bed that will withstand the gnawing of puppy's razor-sharp teeth.

Nowadays, one of the best beds is made of extremely hard plastic. These come with a soft mat for the pup to sleep on. I would say that even though these beds are very hard-wearing, they can still be chewed. On the positive side though, they are easily cleaned, especially if you have a muddy or wet pup.

Plastic bed

Toilet Training

Toilet training should start as soon as you get your new puppy home and most new owners find this task the most difficult than other new owners. As soon as you get home, place the puppy outside in the garden to relieve itself. Stay with him, even if it means taking a little trip around the garden. Get the puppy to familiarise with the area. Make a fuss of it, get down on your knees to the pup's level, clap your hands, the puppy should come running to you. Puppies, under three months of age, have limited bladder control. A puppy usually doesn't know when it wants to go to the toilet until the very last moment when it relieves itself on your kitchen floor! One of the signs you will come familiar with is that you will see your puppy suddenly going round and round in a circle while sniffing the floor. This is perfectly normal, and the sniffing is finding a place or spot that either has already been used before or using this spot as its toilet area. This reaction is what they would normally do in the wild. If your puppy can't find a used spot, he will make his own spot and may keep on using this place because it will have his own scent-mark on.

For preventing accidents in the house, you will need to teach the young puppy the best spot outside you want him to use as a toilet, training the puppy in getting it familiar with this, which will take time as he grows and learns. Keep to a routine, this is very important in the early days, putting the pup outside every time he wants to go to the toilet. He will soon learn by going to the door you will put him outside to relieve himself. Always feed the pup at the same time each day, this again is very important when toilet training. Once you start to understand and observe the signs of your puppy, he will soon let you know when he wants to go to the loo, usually by running to the door or sniffing a particular place or circling round and round on the spot. Your pup may also cry a little while doing so.

The first few weeks, and sometimes months, of owning a puppy are the hardest and the most important. If training is done correctly, this will have an impact on the puppy for the rest of its life. Spending time, effort and patience will pay off. Remember, the puppy does not understand and this is not only a big learning stage for you but also for the puppy as well. A good size cage will be for sleeping and feeding the young puppy, and where you can keep a close eye on him as well. Do not be tempted to give the puppy the full run of the house. At this stage if you do, you can expect accidents to happen and you will need to keep a watchful eye on him at all times. Expect accidents to happen often.

A Few Simple Things to Remember About Your Puppy.

Puppies like to be clean and will very rarely soil where they sleep, i.e. their sleeping area.

At first, your puppy will have very limited bladder control.

Get your puppy into a routine on a daily basis.

When your puppy wakes, he will want to go to the toilet.

After feeding your puppy, he will want to go to the toilet within around half an hour of eating. He will also need to go to the toilet before going to sleep, as well.

Your puppy will need to go to the toilet every hour or so as his bladder is only very small, and they do not have bladder control until they grow.

Most Puppies around 8 to 15 weeks of age will want to go the toilet during the night. Make sure you're able to hear the puppy cry so you can take him out of his cage to relieve himself.

Feed the puppy his supper in his cage. Don't let him out of the cage for at least half an hour. When you do, carry the puppy outside, place the pup on a grassed area or the spot you want him to use as a toilet. Wait for him to go to the toilet before bringing him back in. Some pups relieve themselves quickly, others may take half an hour or so, you will have to be patient.

If your puppy doesn't show any signs of wanting to relieve himself, walk around the garden slowly. Try not to distract him. He should then relieve himself. Walking will get things moving. Your puppy will soon pick a spot to use as a toilet area. Once he uses a spot for the toilet, this can be used for the next time as it will have his smell on it.

Always take the puppy outside first thing in the morning when you let him out of the cage. Always carry the puppy to the outside door. Do not let him run around the house. Puppies always seem to want to relieve themselves the moment they are out of the cage. If you let him run to the door, you can expect an accident to happen. Routine is very important at this early stage in the pup's life. After each play session, take your puppy outside to relieve himself. Once the puppy has relieved himself, put him back in the cage to sleep.

Getting your puppy into a routine for the first month or so is very important. Your puppy should be fed at least three or four times per day. Repeat the same procedure throughout the day. First thing in the morning when the pup wakes up, carry him outside to relieve himself. Let him play for about half an hour so he can stretch his legs and associate you with something nice, then put him back in his cage and feed him his breakfast. After breakfast, carry him again outside to relieve himself, take him to the same spot as before, let the puppy have another half an hour play before putting him back in the cage for a sleep. When he wakes, carry him again outside to relieve himself in the same spot as before, again let him play before feeding his midday meal. Once he has eaten, put him back outside to relieve himself, let him play yet again before having another sleep. This needs to be repeated during the day to get him into a regular routine. It is very important you do the same thing every day; this not only gets the puppy into a routine but will also help when training begins.

Playtimes can be lengthened as the puppy gets older because as he grows, he will require less sleep and will be in more control of his bladder when he wants to go to the toilet. Eventually, the puppy will be letting you know when he needs to go to the toilet. A word of warning, if you ignore the signs when your puppy wants to go to the toilet, he will have an accident! I know this sounds a lot of hard work and it is, but the results will pay off later in a well-house-trained puppy. Keep in mind that some breeds are easier to house train than others. Be patient. Do not scold your puppy if he has an accident.

Keep your puppy's chosen toilet area clean. Make sure you pick up old stools which will eliminate him from eating them. Many puppies will choose a certain spot, if old stools are left, he may refuse to use it and go to the toilet elsewhere instead. Picking up your puppy's stools helps you keep an eye on your puppy's health as well. Stools should be firm and fairly dry, loose or sloppy stools can be an indication of worms and other health problems, digestive problems and stress. The most important thing to remember when house training a puppy is consistency and routine. If you are consistent and do the same thing every time, your puppy will learn very quickly. On the other hand, changing the routine will only confuse the puppy; therefore, the process will take longer in getting the puppy house trained.

Collar and Leads for Your Puppy

There are a variety of soft collars on the market. These include canvas type, leather, soft material and a variety of choke chains.

It is worth considering buying a soft material flat collar. Do not buy a collar that is padded on the inside. The collar must be a good fit but not too loose for the youngster to get stuck in the pup's bottom jaw or a paw caught in the collar. As the youngster grows, you may want to change to a leather collar, and, again, these can be purchased from any good pet shop.

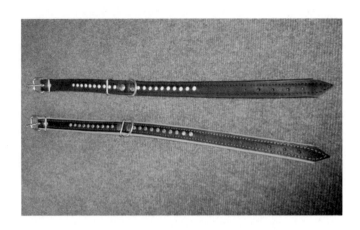

Leather collars

Head halters are another form of collar and can be purchased from most pet suppliers. Head halters fit over the puppy's head and around its nose. The halter is then clipped on to a lead. These halters are great for an older puppy or dog that pulls when walking. It's a quick fix in teaching the pup that it's not allowed to pull forward by giving a gentle tug on the lead when it does, and gently pulling on the lead when the pup pulls, turning the puppy's head inwards towards you. The puppy soon learns that pulling is not acceptable.

Head halter

You will need to purchase a lead for the head halter separately and, again, there are a variety to choose from, made from different materials and come in different sizes depending on how big your puppy is.

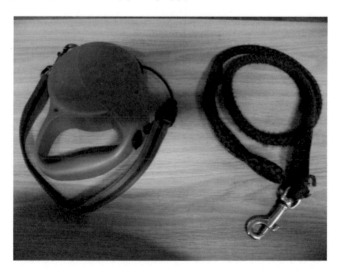

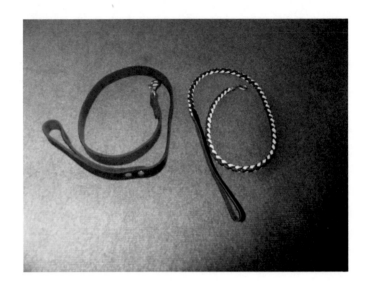

Types of leads

When choosing a lead, make sure it does not have a collar attached to it, these types of leads are usually described as slip leads. There are various types of slip leads on the market, which are an all-in-one collar with lead combined. These are only really suitable for older dogs.

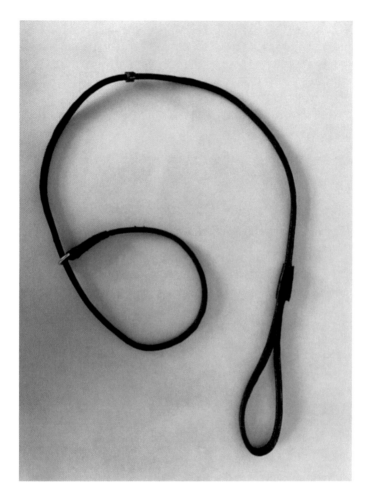

Slip leads

Your puppy will need to wear a collar with a separate lead and the pup will need to get used to having a collar permanently round his neck. Again, leads can be of soft material, leather, chain type leads or a mixture of both. For a youngster, I would stick to a material lead because these are very light in weight and designed not to frighten the young pup.

Talking of leads, there are also extended leads which are on a retractable plastic real which is really useful when training begins. They come in a variety of lengths and just clip onto the youngster's collar. The idea of these leads are as the youngster walks further away, the lead extends and will also retract when getting the youngster to come back to you, and because the lead is sprung loaded, the youngster will not get his legs tied up in the lead.

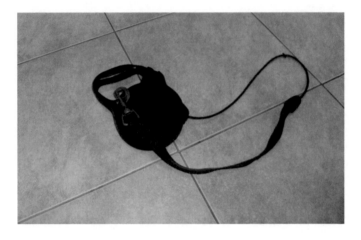

Retractable lead

Chapter 4

Bonding

I am asked many times, "When do I start training a young puppy and at what age?" This is always a difficult question. Many will say, right from the start, the moment you bring the puppy home. One of the main factors you will have to consider is what sort of temperament does your puppy have. Does your puppy have a strong character, or soft nature and is rather shy and timid? You will never get two puppies alike even from the same litter. No two puppies, as I have found over the years, can be trained in the same way. Like human beings, they are individuals. The early days, as with a child, are the most important. Bonding with the puppy is the most important part in the earlier months of a puppy's life. I like to call this the play training stage, where you will build a bond with your puppy. In return, the puppy will begin to trust you and associate you being the pack leader. You may have to determine if your puppy is a bold, headstrong and inquisitive pup, or is the puppy a soft natured, affectionate or shy type that may need bringing out of himself. Like every puppy, they are all different in many ways and will have to be trained according to their character. You will need to watch the reaction of your pup with people, other dogs, noises and the general way the puppy investigates his surroundings. All of these things are important in making your mind up as to what sort of temperament the young pup has and how you are going to train it, and in what way. Whatever type of nature the pup has, you must remember that the impact in the early days of training will have an effect on the youngsters reactions later on as the pup grows, not only with you, but with other people and dogs it comes into contact with. Again, in the early stages, if a pup is mishandled in training, this will also have a dramatic effect on its nature as well and the way it responds to you and others.

Puppies and dogs, no matter what age, bond with human beings during the time they spend with them. They can bond with each member of the family and this will be in different ways, but they can form a stronger bond with one individual person within the family. Usually, this is because one individual interacts more with the puppy and the puppy then associates that person with something nice. The puppy will also look up to this person as being its pack leader just as they would in the wild. There would be many dogs but only one dog in the pack would be the dominant pack leader that they would grow to trust and would protect them from predators. This will form the bond between the human being and the puppy or dog and with careful observation of the puppy and how its mind thinks and understanding the basics of training. How the owner reacts to a situation will influence the bonding process during the first few months of the puppy's life. The puppy needs to be confident and have trust in its owner. Once the bond has been created the puppy will respect its new owner's as being its pack leader in what he is telling the puppy to do. Not only puppies but dogs also need to have confidence and trust in the owner's abilities, thus building a strong bond between the two individuals in order to be able to train the pup to the standard you want.

Bonding

Creating a strong bond between the owner and the puppy is extremely important and must start from the moment the new puppy joins the family. Once the initial settling-in period is achieved, forming the bond will give trust and confidence, and increase the strength of the relationship between the two of you.

Key Points of Bonding

1. Spend quality time on a daily basis giving the puppy plenty of attention.
2. Play with your puppy at a certain time of the day making the play training fun. Your puppy will then associate you with something nice.
3. Never raise your voice, always keep a gentle tone with your puppy.
4. Get other members of the family to play with your puppy. This will give him confidence not just in you but with different people.
5. The bonding process does not happen overnight and may take time depending on the puppy's nature. The puppy

will grow stronger each day in trusting you and the relationship you build between you both.

All this will develop a solid foundation and build trust between you and the puppy. From this, you will soon learn to read the puppy's mind and his body language, with certain situations when they arise and address and respond accordingly to them. For example, in a situation where the puppy is greeted by a strange dog or person, the puppy may show signs of fear towards the other dog or person. You must quickly be able to read the puppy's body language and lead the puppy quickly, but quietly, away from the situations the puppy finds as a threat. You will reinforce the position that you are the strong pack leader. The puppy will learn to trust you and this will also strengthen the bond between the two of you. The puppy will also look to you as being his pack leader, and this is a natural instinct in the wild as there would always be a dominant leader leading the pack.

Important key points to remember are communication and trust between you and your puppy. This is needed for the basis of training. The whole purpose of any training with your puppy is to make the puppy aware that you are in control of him as the pack leader and what you are asking the puppy to do. This must be done without being domineering or forceful. If not, the young puppy will shy away and become frightened. You cannot set the foundations or achieve this if you make the puppy fearful of you. The puppy needs to be set certain boundaries and interactions and play training which must be enforced on a daily basis. You need to be understanding, fair but firm and consistent. Many puppies cannot cope with owners and other members of the family with high levels of arguments and raised voices, emotions and continuous stress or children shouting and screaming. You will not be able to create a strong bond if the puppy is constantly receiving mixed messages on what is or what isn't allowed. This will only confuse the puppy leading to the breakdown of communication and the bonding process, which may leave the puppy frightened and unsure of what is being asked of him.

Assessing the Puppy's Nature: The Bold Puppy

Assessing the bold puppy, the bold puppy is usually of the headstrong type and will want to do things on his own. The pup may not take much notice of you. You may find because of the puppy's bold nature that he will be more inquisitive and, at first, it will be difficult to attract his attention. This may lead to problems trying to keep the pup's attention on you; however, this is easily solved.

Pick a space, maybe the back garden somewhere the pup is familiar with no distractions. Make sure it's just you and the puppy. Have a couple of tennis balls in your pocket, lay on the floor and call the pup by his name. At the same time, gently roll the ball so he can see the ball. Again, call the pup's name and gently roll the second ball. The pup will soon respond. If the pup gets distracted by something else, move out towards the pup and give him a gentle poke with your finger to catch his attention. You can also give the pup a puppy treat. Once you have caught the pup's attention, back away and call his name again, roll the tennis ball towards him. When the pup runs towards you, give him plenty of fuss. Whatever you do, do not shout at the pup or flap your arms about in frustration if you cannot gain his attention. This will only frighten him; no puppy will want to come to you if you're constantly raising your voice. The idea is to keep the training sessions short just to five minutes. If not, once the pup becomes tired, he will lose concentration. Always make sure you keep everything close and never let the pup get more than five feet in front of you. On a very reluctant strong-headed pup, I will usually reward him with puppy treats when he comes to me. Once you have the pup responding to you, the puppy treat can be replaced with praise and fuss instead. On a daily basis keep practising these training sessions. Not only will the pup look forward to playing with the ball, he will also associate you with something nice, play and plenty of fuss. The pup will quickly learn what you are telling him to do and also learn to trust you as his pack leader.

The Soft Puppy

On the other hand, the soft-natured puppy is the complete opposite of the bold puppy. The pup will need to be stimulated to boost his confidence and gain trust in you as his pack leader. In the same way as with the bold puppy, get down to the pup's level or lay on the floor. By doing this, he will not feel intimated by your height. Roll a tennis ball in front of the pup. You will find with a soft-natured pup that he will not want to venture and may back off or run to you. He will only want to remain close to you, but still, make a fuss of him using a soft tone in your voice. Again, at this stage, it doesn't matter if the pup shows no interest in the ball. The pup may want to stay close to you. Be careful not to put too much pressure on the youngster at this stage. Softer-natured puppies may take longer to train because they lack confidence and are unsure; just keep the lessons short, five minutes at a time until the pup's confidence grows.

Many people will tell you what you should and shouldn't do when you start to train a puppy; for instance, they may tell you, "Don't let children play or throw things for the puppy." This, to me, is the most important stage in the pup's life. You should not deprive the puppy in the early days of socialising and interacting. Puppies are always drawn to children. They should be able to play and mix with children; in turn, they will soon learn to trust and bond. If they are not allowed contact with children, this may lead to barking and growling at children in the latter days to come.

The onset of play training should always be fun for a young puppy, and unbeknown to the puppy, this is when training actually begins. At the same time, the puppy will start to bond with you as his pack leader. He will start to learn to trust you and want to be with you. Play training starts in many different forms. This could be, playing with him rolling a ball in a room or the garden or playing with his favourite toy.

Calling the Puppy by Name

When calling the puppy by his name, you will need to get down to the puppy's level, and the reason why I say this is because the puppy will not feel intimidated by your height. Many softer-natured puppies may show signs of being nervous. Just kneeling down will help in getting the puppy to respond and build trust in you as well, thus creating a bond between the two of you.

Getting down to the puppy's level

Roll a ball or the pup's favourite toy in front of your puppy. When your puppy runs after the ball, gently call the pup by his name and pat your knees or clap your hands at the same time. Still keep calling your puppy by his name, have a treat ready to hand to entice him to come back to you. When your puppy gets close to you, reward him with the treat and plenty of fuss. Your puppy will soon associate being called and coming to you with something positive, a treat and plenty of fuss.

Repeat the training sessions several times. The pup will soon put together his name being called with something nice, coming back to you for a treat and some fuss.

Tempting a puppy

You have to make it as tempting as possible to get the young pup's attention. Keep practising every day with him for five minutes each time. He will soon get used to being called by his name and will eagerly want to come back to you.

Don't forget, in the early days it's most important to get down to the pup's level for two reasons.

1. The height of a person may intimate the young pup. He will feel more secure if you are at his level, which will make him come to you less afraid, especially if he's a softer-natured pup.
2. It will also stop a young pup from jumping up at you, creating a bad habit later when he's starting to mature into an adult dog.
3. Once the puppy is fully confident and doesn't feel intimidated by your height, you can then stand up normal and call the puppy in your usual way. Anyone play training with your puppy should be supervised and should use the same technique and commands as you do. There is nothing more annoying when someone comes home, or visits, the first thing the dog does is jumps up at you or another person, or when you call him, especially if the dog has muddy feet. This is a hard habit to break. If you allow a young pup in the early days to jump up, this may also lead to a

further habit later, i.e. jumping up at doors in the house as well.

Play Training the Basics of Training
Teaching Your Puppy to Sit

You can easily start training your puppy when play training begins, getting your puppy to sit. For instance, when it's feed time, you can teach the puppy to sit before allowing him to eat his food, just by gently holding his collar at the back of his neck, gently push his bottom down to the floor together with a gentle voice command 'SIT'.

Again, when your puppy has sat for a few seconds, praise him and give him a treat, followed by his food. If you do this every time before he is fed, he will get used to this, the puppy will quickly associate sitting to your voice command, he will associate this with something nice, which will be his food. Don't make the puppy sit for too long; he will only lose concentration and will start to become naughty because he wants his food. Make the puppy sit for just a few seconds only.

Do not be tempted to start at this stage, making the pup stay or try and reinforce commands, the pup is not ready for.

If you do, the pup will just crumble under pressure at this tender age. This is only the start of play training which builds the bond between you and the pup and builds his confidence and trust in you. Your puppy needs to be able to play and grow confidently and enjoy being with you. He will quickly learn and associate play training with something nice and will look forward to being with you. This is the very start of the gradual process of training and the future ahead. The main objectives of play training are to start the bonding process, getting the pup's attention so you are able to assess his nature and temperament. The puppy also needs to feel confident and trust you as well. This will bring enjoyment not just for you but also for the pup as well.

Key Points to Remember

1. Do not over-stimulate your puppy with too much playing training.
2. Don't chase after your puppy or tease him when playing with him.
3. Don't give your puppy too many different toys. Stick to just half a dozen toys.
4. Don't play fight or wrestle with your puppy especially when he is playing with his toys. If your puppy is from one of the larger breeds, this could cause problems later as the youngster grows into an adult dog and may show signs of aggression.
5. Always have a variety of toys for your puppy to play with, which should include a selection of chew toys and interactive toys as well, which will help stimulate the puppy's brain while playing with them.
6. Do not let your puppy play with toys that squeak. This will only make him want to chew them more and more. When your puppy starts the teething stage, it will only encourage him to chew other unwanted items in the hope that they squeak.

7. Always teach your puppy that his toys are acceptable to plays with. The moment he starts to play, i.e. with your shoes, replace immediately with one of his toys.

8. Make sure during play periods with your puppy you use a gentle but firm tone in your voice when trying to gain the pup's attention, do not shout at him. The young puppy needs to understand that you are in control as the pack leader.

9. Choosing toys that squeak may overexcite your puppy. He will constantly want to bite the toy which will excite the puppy even more.

10. Remember when play training with your puppy, never hover over him. This will only teach your puppy bad habits such as jumping up, nipping and biting, barking, and becoming overexcited when playing with him. Standing with a tall posture and plenty of eye contact will communicate to your puppy that you are the pack leader and you are in control.

11. Keep play training games short to ten minutes, three or four times a day and at the same times during the day to get your puppy into a routine.

12. Try to teach your puppy during play training sessions such as teaching him his name, calling him to come back to you, sit, fetch, and the command 'No' when he has done wrong. These simple commands can all be achieved during play training, and with plenty of time and patience your puppy will grow more confident while you're play training with him, associating you as his pack leader someone your puppy can trust.

Chapter 5

The Horrid Chewing Stage

Puppies begin to cut their milk teeth around three weeks of age; they have approximately twenty-eight milk teeth. When a puppy loses its milk teeth, these will be replaced by adult teeth. As the milk teeth push through the gums and erupt, this causes irritation, itching and great pain to the young puppy. These small milk teeth are razor-sharp and often the mother dog will reject the pup from feeding due to the discomfort when the puppy is suckling. When the puppy is around four to five months of age, these milk teeth will eventually be replaced by adult teeth. In total, the puppy will have around forty-two teeth. This is when full chewing begins for the puppy. The extent of the chewing may vary considerably depending on the breed and the nature of the pup. By the time the puppy is around eight to twelve months of age, the puppy should have a full set of adult teeth. This is when the next stage of chewing begins the adolescent chewing. At this stage, it does not mean the chewing will stop, the young puppy will start to explore other things to chew. As the teeth begin to set into the jawbone and the gums begin to mature and harden around the teeth, it will again cause pain and discomfort, which will make the youngster chew even more. Basically, the chewing stage is driven by the discomfort of the teeth setting into the puppy's jawbone, and the puppy's discomfort creates the desire to chew and also learn about his environment and other things to stimulate him as well. Usually, by the time the pup reaches an adult at around two years of age, the chewing stage may decrease and stop.

During the early stages of chewing, if the chewing becomes excessive, the puppy can be confined in a caged pen in order to try and control the chewing, and also reduce the pup's razor knife teeth chewing something that you don't want him to chew, i.e. your shoes. Once the puppy gets to adolescent stage, the chewing may not stop, and, quite often, the painful chewing later will be replaced by chewing its environment and the surroundings the puppy lives in. If your puppy is not stimulated and becomes bored or left isolated, chewing may get worse. Puppies learn from exploring what is around them, which causes them to chew, and as long as you keep the learning behaviour from becoming a habit, your puppy should outgrow the chewing stage at some point eventually over time.

Some particular breeds such as Labradors and working dogs are more prone to chewing than other breeds. These particular breeds may chew up to about eighteen months of age, even two years and even longer. If a puppy is left alone for long periods of time, this can and will make the puppy chew more and more. One of the biggest factors of excessive chewing is boredom which can become a habit. Like all youngsters, they will need to be stimulated with hard toys. You can buy virtually indestructible toys from most pet supermarkets. These toys are designed for razor-sharp teeth. They come in various sizes depending on the size of your puppy or adult dog.

Make sure you always buy toys that do not squeak when chewed. If toys squeak this will only make the pup chew even more which you don't want, especially if you are wanting to train the pup as a working dog later on.

When chewing starts, there are helpful things you can do to try and alleviate chewing unwanted items in the house. If the puppy has to be left alone, put him in a cage i.e. a collapsible travel cage. This will reduce the chewing. Buy hard indestructible toys. There are a selection on the market that are made for even the worst dog chewer. They will last a lot longer than the average dog toy. Give your puppy a variety of toys on a regular basis to prevent boredom.

Plastic toys

Do not leave the pup alone in the house or outside unsupervised. I have known dogs chew wallpaper; one, in particular, was left unattended. When left by its owner for three hours, the puppy found it great fun stripping paper off the wall, also chewing the skirting boards and door and anything else it could get its teeth into.

The owner was not impressed, nor did they find it amusing either. The puppy literally demolished their newly decorated bathroom. Do not leave shoes, slippers etc. or any child's toys around the house. If you do, they may get chewed and partially eaten as well. This will only cause temptation for the puppy to want to chew even more.

If you keep the pup occupied enough, this will help the pup through the chewing stage. Again, spend some time each day play training with the pup. This will help to stimulate it. Give the puppy some hard toys to chew on. Afterwards, the puppy should sleep for a few hours.

One word of warning once the chewing stage starts: make sure the pup's bed is solid enough to take its razor-sharp teeth. There will be very little soft bedding on the market that will withstand the chewing so look very carefully at what you buy. Do your homework and read the label first. If not, you may find in a matter of hours of buying a new bed for your puppy that the bed has been partially chewed and eaten.

Some breeds and crossbreeds can be the most dreadful chewers and will never grow out of the chewing stage. Many hunting, sporting and working breeds such as retrievers, spaniels and setters are more prone to chewing than other breeds. Terriers, active dogs with a bolder nature who bore more easily, often chew out of pure boredom. Some breeds never grow out of the chewing stage and will almost try anything to get their teeth into when they are unsupervised and left alone.

There are a number of small breed of dogs i.e. French Bulldog, Pug, Boston Terrier, Shih Tzu, Cavalier King Charles Spaniel and, especially, those with rounded skulls and pushed in faces (brachycephalic breeds). Some of these breeds can retain a small number of baby teeth while cutting their adult teeth. Once the adult teeth have come through, this will usually cause misalignment of the teeth along with tooth decay because the youngster has not only got his adult teeth but also has retained some puppy teeth as well. This can cause the youngster to chew into its adult years due to the fact that the mouth is overcrowded and the discomfort it causes.

Ways to Manage Chewing

You can manage your puppy's chewing by providing your puppy with toys and chews, hard indestructible toys, bones and other speciality items designed for teething puppies. Some items, in particular, that I have found over the years and are very good and are virtually indestructible are ram's horn, buffalo and stag horns. All of them are very hard and even for the worst chewer of all time, will last just about forever. This is money well spent.

Buffalo horns

The added bonus of buffalo horns can also be filled with dog biscuits, which will encourage the puppy to chew the horns. They can be purchased from any good pet supplier. As the puppy becomes more mature, especially during the adolescent chewing stage, you can teach the pup what he can and cannot chew. During the earlier stages of chewing, put the puppy in his cage. When you are unable to supervise him or he is left unattended, he will then be out of reach to whatever he wants to chew on when left alone.

Simple Ways to Distract Your Puppy from Chewing

Step 1

Clap your hands or stamp your feet on the floor and say 'NO, NO' in a firm voice. When you catch your pup chewing on something inappropriate, i.e. a kitchen chair, you will have to catch him in the act first; otherwise, he will not be able to associate NO with your command. This will startle him and will be a shock tactic and should stop the pup in his tracks. As soon as you have the pup's attention, show him a toy, a bone or a food-stuffed dog toy. Praise him when he shows interest in playing with the toy or bone. Do this each time you catch him chewing something; you don't want him to chew. Over time, he will associate his toys with something nice.

Step 2

If the puppy's persistent chewing gets out of control and you are finding it difficult to manage, you can buy a commercial product called Cribox. This is used for horses to stop them from chewing their wooden stable doors, which is sometimes caused by boredom. In most cases, this will stop the pup from chewing a particular item due to the fact that Cribox is a brown paste and has a horrible, nasty taste. You can also put some of this on your woodwork that the puppy persistently chews. This should stop the puppy from chewing. If you can't buy any Cribox, you can buy other types of deterrents from most pet store designed specifically for puppy's and dogs that chew. Make sure you always test the product first, to see if your puppy dislikes it, because it may not have a strong enough taste to deter your puppy and he may continue with his chewing habits. Firstly, spray or smear the product on a tissue or old cloth and try to encourage your puppy to smell it. If the pup shakes his head or coughs and spits while smelling it, you can then apply it daily to the items you want to protect. But remember, your puppy will then find yet another bit of wood or something else to chew on elsewhere. The process will be slow and ongoing until he grows out of the chewing stage. Be aware though when using products like this, you must read the small print on the back. Cribox is ideal for use in kennels and runs where everything is made of wood. As with any product you buy, always seek independent advice from your veterinary before use.

Step 3

Confine your puppy when you cannot supervise him or when he is left alone for long periods of time, to prevent him from doing any further damage by chewing.

Put him in a cage or a dog pen, give him very hard indestructible toys, or a hard bone or food-stuffed dog toy to keep him occupied. He can settle down and sleep afterwards.

Put your Puppy in a cage or puppy pen while unsupervised

Step 4

Stimulate your puppy mentally and physically on a daily basis four or five times a day. Your puppy will be less likely to get bored and less likely to start looking for things he can chew when left alone. After play sessions the pup will normally sleep. As part of the pup's play training sessions, take your puppy for short walks play with him with his favourite toys, throw things for him and teach him to fetch, let him run around the garden so he can tire himself out. Again, he will then sleep. Providing plenty of different toys for your puppy to play with and with regular ten minute play sessions will stimulate him mentally and physically. You will then find that when left alone unsupervised, he will be stimulated mentally and physically.

Stool Eating

Many owners of a puppy will find stool eating disgusting. There are many different reasons why puppies and dogs eat their own stools. Some puppies may start eating stools while still in the litter with their mother. This stems from the strong pack animal instinct in them not only in the mother but also in the puppies as well. In the wild, the mother will eat the stools of her puppies to keep the den clean and also protect the puppies from predators that might be drawn to their smell. Not only this, when puppies are born, they have no control over their bladders nor their bowel movements either. The mother will lick her puppies and by doing this, will stimulate the puppy to go to the toilet. Just because dogs are domesticated today, they still have this strong pack animal instinct in them to protect their litter from predators that may harm or even kill them. This is the main reason why the mother of her puppies will keep the den and surrounding area clean. From the onset of the puppies being born, the mother will eat the stools until the puppies are weaned. As the puppies grow and mature within the litter, they will copy the mother and will also copy the other puppies as well. If one puppy eats its own stools, the other puppies will copy. This is totally natural and is a part of a puppy learning by watching what the other puppies and dogs do because of their inquisitive nature.

The mother usually stops eating her puppies' stools and cleaning up after them once the puppies are on solid food, but because puppies learn very quickly, they may still continue to eat their stools until they become more mature. This is all part of learning as they grow and mature, along with the natural puppy curiosity that leads them to smell and taste. Dogs do not have taste buds like human beings, but they taste their food through smell.

Another factor as to why some puppies eat their own stools: If a puppy is left alone, it may eat its own stool or other dog's stool out of boredom, or there could be other underlying health issues that causes stool eating. If in doubt, consult your veterinary surgeon. Though stool eating, known as coprophagy, is disgusting for the owner, it is quite normal behaviour for a puppy to eat its own stools, but if the cause is not addressed, it may become a recurring bad habit as the puppy grows into an adult dog and will continue to eat not only its own stools but also other dog's stools as well. It is not uncommon to find puppies in the litter eating other puppies' stools because they copy each other in order for them to learn. If puppies are receiving a well-balanced diet rich in nutrients, they should grow out of this type of behaviour quickly. However, some do not, and if it continues, you may want to check if your puppy has any deficiencies in order for this to be ruled out first. Always feed your puppy on a good quality complete puppy food that is high in protein, minerals, vitamins and other nutrients, which the pup needs for normal growth.

Things to watch out for

Any signs your puppy may be suffering from:

- Poor digestion.
- Poor growth.
- Weight loss or not putting on enough weight.
- Diarrhoea, watery stools and may have undigested food in the stools.
- Vomiting
- Coughing.

If you see any of these symptoms, consult your Veterinarian as there may be underlying problems which, if left untreated, may become a serious issue.

Other Reasons for Stool Eating

There are several reasons why puppies eat their own or other puppy's stools.

Poor digestion: Your puppy may not be digesting his food properly. The food may be of poor quality and not high enough in protein having low nutrient digestibility which will result in the puppy's digestive system not being able to digest food in the normal way. When the food passes through the gut, it is still undigested, which makes it more palatable for the puppy to eat. Or the puppy may have a problem with his digestive system. In a nutshell, when the puppy eats his stools, it tastes pretty much the same food as the food he has just eaten, purely because it hasn't been digested properly. Switching to a higher protein food can solve this problem, and it must be specially formulated for puppies. Most large pet stores sell a wide variety of high protein good quality puppy food and will also give you some advice as to what requirements your puppy needs.

Hunger: From the onset of puppies being born, they must be fed at regular intervals three to four times a day and not left hungry. Leaving them hungry will only lead to stool eating, which, again, is another natural reaction like when in the wild to fight for survival. An infestation of worms and other intestinal parasites can and will drain nutrients from the puppy's system, causing the pup to be weak and hungry. Puppies may eat anything that appears edible including their own stools and other dog stools as well.

Boredom: This can be a cause for stool eating. If a puppy is left alone for long periods of time and without stimulation, the pup may eat his own stools. If the puppy is left to his own devices, it may form a recurring bad habit that it may never grow out of, purely because it has formed a bad habit.

They like the taste of it: Some puppies, and adult dogs, will eat their own stool because they like the taste of it. All you can do is to try and prevent the puppy from continuing to eat his own stools, by trying to distract him by picking the stools up as quickly as possible.

Preventing Stool Eating

To try and prevent stool eating, make sure your puppy is getting plenty of play training sessions, taking him for short walks, which will stimulate him and gives him the attention he needs. When your puppy is left on his own, he will be more inclined to sleep instead of feeling lonely and bored and consequently eating his stools out of frustration. Puppies need to sleep a lot while they are growing. Stimulating your puppy helps in maintaining the routine.

The best cure in preventing stool eating is to clean up after your puppy. If you don't, the temptation for your puppy to eat the stools or even play with them, in time, will become habit-forming.

Food

Another way is to distract your puppy with food in an attempt to prevent him from eating his stools. Clap your hand when you catch him in the act of stool eating. If he does respond to you, give him a reward, a small puppy biscuit. He will eventually associate the biscuit with clapping your hands and his name being called with something nice a treat. If you can't distract him, say 'NO, NO' in a stern but firm voice and put the pup on a lead immediately.

Always keep your puppy on a lead when you take him out for a walk. This will prevent him from eating his stools or other dog's stools as well. If your puppy does eat other dog stools, he may come into contact with parasites. These parasites can be transmitted once eaten. The pup may run the risk of being unwell. If you catch your puppy sniffing at a stool, pull him away in the opposite direction and say 'NO, NO' in a stern voice.

Adding additives to your puppy's food.

There are products on the market nowadays that can be easily purchased in most pet stores which help prevent puppies from stool eating. When added to their food, the additive gives off a very unpleasant and unappealing smell which deters the puppy from eating stools. A small piece of pineapple can also have the same effect when added to the pup's food as well. You can also purchase various types of sprays that are available in most pet stores. When the spray is applied over old stools, it discourages the puppy or dog from eating them.

A high-quality puppy food

Your puppy will need to be on a highly digestible puppy food, made purely for puppies. If your puppy is not on a high protein food, he will not digest his food properly, and it will go through his system too quickly, which will result in undigested food that will come out the other end. This will make stool eating for him much more appealing to eat. Whereas a high quality, highly digestible puppy food will take longer for the pup's body to digest and will be less palatable when it comes out the other end, and he will be less likely to eat the stools.

Increase the amount of daily exercise,

Give your puppy several sessions throughout the day's play training. Give him plenty of attention. He will be more interested in wanting to sleep afterwards when left alone. Make sure you get into the habit of cleaning up stools immediately and to keep temptation out of the pup's reach. Always keep your pup on a lead. Do not be tempted to let him off the lead when taking your puppy out for a walk, and remember, if your puppy shows signs of wanting to stool eat, keep him on a lead when he wants to go to the toilet. If you let him off the lead, he may be tempted to eat not only his own stools but other dogs' stools as well.

Most puppies eventually grow out of stool eating, but some puppies never get out of the habit and grow into adult dogs, still eating stools and other stools such as cat and horse stools as well. The only thing you can do is keep a watchful eye and clear up after him. If you cannot stop the stool eating when out walking your puppy or dog, another alternative you may want to consider is, you can purchase from most pet stores dog muzzles. They come in various sizes. They simply fit over the dog's nose and under the jaw and clip together behind the back of the dog's head. The dog can still breathe but cannot pick anything up in its mouth and attempt to eat it. Putting a muzzle on an adult dog that persistently tries to eat stools and other items when out on short walks will eliminate what the dog eats. If you always keep your puppy or dog on a lead when out walking, this stops the temptation.

Chapter 6

Socialising Your Puppy

It is very important during the first year of a dog's life. It encounters being socialised as much as possible not only with other dogs but children and adults as well. Socialising during the first year will make all the difference to the puppy's character and temperament. Taking time to socialise the puppy will result in the puppy enjoying the company of people and different situations. The puppy will soon learn to associate these experiences with something nice. This is the most important part of the puppy's life and between three weeks to nine months of age, a puppy must get used to meeting as many different people, children, situations and other dogs as possible and be able to interact with them as well. The puppy will have to be introduced to different sounds when out and about on short walks as well. This is crucial in the early days of the pup's development, which will help the puppy grow, learn and develop. Between the ages of five to twelve weeks is the most important in particular because a puppy will approach anything or anybody willingly and usually without fear. Whereas the older puppy that hasn't had different experiences with people, children and other dogs will approach with caution and may show signs of anxiety, nervousness and fear. Meeting people and socialising should be the most important and enjoyable part of your puppy's growing up and training sessions. The more people your puppy meets and plays with, the more friendly and sociable your puppy will become. He will associate all good experiences with something nice. The younger your puppy is, the easier it will be to socialise him with different situations, whereby leaving the socialising until the puppy is older will make him more nervous. Your puppy may become more cautious when faced with new and different experiences. The early weeks are extremely important. Most puppies will approach any situation without fear. This is because, as puppies get older, they become more cautious when faced with new situations and experiences, which is part of their inbuilt animal pack instinct in them.

Socialising with People

Getting Your Puppy Used to Socialising with People

Taking the time to socialise your puppy and getting him familiar, interacting with men, women, children and all types of situations. Some puppies may react to a man's voice because the tone is much deeper than a woman's voice. All meetings should be a positive experience for your puppy. It's important that your puppy does not feel overwhelmed. Some puppies are cautious of certain physical features. This could be someone wearing a hat, wearing a pair of glasses, a long coat, someone in a uniform or a child pulling a facial expression. If your puppy shows any signs of being cautious or being anxious, whatever the situation is try and turn the negative into a positive reaction. For example, a stranger has just put their hand straight out to fuss your puppy. The puppy's reaction is, he instantly backs off and shows signs of being nervous and tries to run away. To rectify the situation, ask the stranger to crouch or kneel down at the same time look away from the puppy and not to give the puppy any eye contact whatsoever. Let the puppy sniff the stranger. The puppy will be reassured that no harm will come to him. Once the puppy shows no sign of being nervous, walk the puppy away from the stranger. Giving the puppy direct eye contact will make the pup class this as a threat and it will back off. In the wild, if a strange dog enters another dog's territory, he will either back away or fight. This is due to eye contact being made by both dogs. Dogs in the wild are very territorial, especially if a strange dog is trying to enter the pack for leadership and dominance and will automatically go into fight or flight mode. Your puppy should approach a new person, rather than the other way around. This way, you can judge how your puppy is feeling and if he is confident meeting someone unfamiliar. If your puppy does start to feel cautious when meeting a new person, you can try gently talking to your puppy. People and children find it very tempting when puppies are small, wanting to pick puppies up and fuss them. Your puppy will automatically class this as a threat and because of this, will frighten the young puppy, especially if your puppy has a shy and timid nature. Do not let people pick your puppy up or reach out to touch him until you know he is confident and shows no signs of fear. Observe your puppy constantly for signs of anxiety or being overwhelmed. If things get too much, remove your puppy from the situation. Remember a young puppy will tire easily, so keep all encounters, interactions and walks short so your puppy can sleep. Avoid bad experiences as this will have an effect on your puppy as he grows into an adult dog. Young puppies, as they grow and mature, can get into trouble easily and can encounter bad experiences from this, so try and prevent unpleasant things happening while your puppy is growing. If unpleasant situations happen, they will not only have an effect on his nature but also have an effect on his confidence. He will be less likely to want to interact and shy away. A good way when you are socialising your pup with people, even strangers, is to have some puppy biscuits in your pocket. Every time your puppy interacts, give him a biscuit. He will soon learn to interact with people. He will associate this with something nice, a biscuit. If he shows signs of being cautious around a particular person, get the person to give him a biscuit but make sure they do not give your puppy any eye contact. Your puppy will soon learn not to be cautious and will associate the experience with something nice.

Meeting people

Socialising with Other Dogs

Socialising your puppy with other dogs is extremely important. You want your puppy eventually to interact with other dogs showing no signs of aggression or fear. For an adult dog that was not socialised when it was a puppy, it will be much more difficult to socialise it as it gets older. You will have to introduce your puppy on a lead at first, preferably with a single dog, gradually at first building your puppy's confidence on a daily basis. Make sure you give your puppy plenty of praise when he has been good. If he behaves badly and starts to bark, gets excited or jumps up at the other dog, say the 'NO' command with a firm tone in your voice and pull him away from the other dog. An adult dog that has never been socialised with another dog may show signs of aggression, but with time and patience and dedication, can be taught to behave well in the same way with other dogs as with a puppy.

There is nothing worse than having an aggressive puppy or dog that barks, yaps, growls and jumps all over when it sees or comes in contact with other dogs, passing vehicles or people. The puppy will have to learn to mix and socialise calmly and not be afraid. In the wild, their natural reaction would be to bark, growl and warn off the intruder, showing aggression at the same time. This will enable them to protect their territory and hierarchy of the pack leader. Puppies will also have a strong natural ability to copy other puppies and dogs. This is part of their learning and growing up into an adult dog not only in the wild but today as well. We have domesticated these animals, so in a sense they pick up on our feelings and look at us as their pack leader for dominance. They also learn to trust us in what we are telling them to do.

When socialising the puppy with other dogs, do not let the puppy off the lead or let it charge around senselessly out of control. This may be tempting when you're in a field with your puppy or someone's garden. If you do allow this to happen, the puppy could easily get injured because the bones and joints have still not fully developed. Secondly, when off the lead, the puppy may become overexcited when meeting a bigger dog. The other dog may feel overwhelmed and threatened by the puppy's excitement and will either snap or show signs of aggression to warn the puppy off. The older dog may even attack the young puppy. Always have your puppy on a short lead when approaching an unfamiliar dog. If he shows any signs of being nervous, reassure him with plenty of praise, and talk to your puppy calmly with a gentle tone in your voice. If your puppy gets excited, he will usually want to play with the older dog, but at this stage, do not allow this to happen until they have become accustomed to one another.

Introducing your puppy to a new dog

You should start introducing your puppy with a familiar dog at first. You may have a friend or someone in the family with a dog that has already been well socialised and has an easy-going temperament with other dogs. Take your puppy on short walks together. This will build the puppy's confidence. If you choose the same place to take them for walks on a regular basis, the puppy will soon learn and become eager to go out for a walk and again associate this with something nice. When you do go out on short walks, keep the puppy apart from the other dog until they get used to one another. If they remain well behaved, you can then allow them to sniff each other gently.

Keep your Puppy on a short lead

If there are any signs of aggressive behaviour, separate them immediately; talk to your puppy in a gentle tone until you have reassured him.

Once they have accustomed themselves to one another, you will notice after a while when the puppy meets the other dog, their tails will start to wag. When you are confident, they have settled to one another at this point, you can let them play together off the lead in a small confined area such as a back garden, where you have control if anything untoward happens.

Continue to introduce your puppy on a regular basis in the same way. When approaching a strange dog for the first time, keep the puppy at a distance. Over the next couple of weeks, you will find that the pup's confidence will grow towards other dogs when out walking. If your puppy does show signs of being nervous, you can stand between your puppy and the other dog, just in case there are any signs of aggressiveness towards your puppy. Eventually, over a period of time, every dog that your puppy meets when out walking, he will remain calm and not feel intimidated and overwhelmed or threatened. An older dog will rarely attack a puppy under six months of age, but it's better to be cautious in the early days.

Get the puppy thoroughly used to socialising with other dogs on a regular basis by taking him for daily walks. Try and stick to the same route so he gets accustomed to that particular walk, before moving on to somewhere different. This will not only build the puppy's confidence but he will also associate the walk with something nice, especially if you have a puppy of a more nervous and timid nature. Once his confidence grows meeting other dogs, your pup will eventually associate this with something nice.

Socialising Your Puppy with Children

It's important you get your puppy used to socialising with children as soon as possible, and this must be done at a very young age. A critical time for your puppy is between seven to sixteen weeks of age. During this time, they can absorb a great deal of information and are eager to learn, plus they are extremely inquisitive. Puppies are far less fearful at this young age and tend to respond to new situations better than that of an older puppy.

A puppy will be easier going than an adult dog when socialising. If your puppy encounters a positive experience when socialising with children, he will associate this encounter with something nice.

On the other hand, if he encounters a bad experience, this may have a damaging effect as he grows into an adult dog and may class every child he sees as a threat which, later, may turn into aggressive behaviour as the puppy grows. As puppies mature and grow into adult dogs, some may change and become wary of children. This is perfectly natural especially if the dog is of a more softer and timid nature. This is because they do not see children as an adult, many dogs see children as a threat because they jump and move around quickly shouting, screaming, throwing their arms and legs around. Many dogs find this sort of behaviour intimidating and will class all children as a threat especial those dogs that have a timid nature.

When introducing your puppy to children they are not accustomed to, the child should be supervised at all times by an adult. Always have the puppy on a lead so you are in control. Once the puppy feels at ease, the child can then give the puppy a treat.

The puppy will soon associate being in the company of a child with something nice, a treat.

Do not let children run up to your puppy. This will only make him fearful, which may make him snap at the child. The first few occasions, ask the child to stand still, look away and not look directly into the puppy's eyes. If your puppy appears calm with no fear, the child can give him a puppy biscuit. If he starts to wag his tail, the child can look at your puppy giving him a biscuit at the same. Your puppy will soon associate the child with something positive. Gradually walking the young puppy up to a child, letting him smell the child, will reassure the young puppy, the child is not a threat. Usually, if this is done on a regular basis with no eye contact from the child, the young pup will become reassured that the child is not a threat and the puppy will again associate the child with something positive.

Some puppies are nervous of children, and the reason for this is unknowingly that when the child first makes contact with a puppy, the child looks directly into the puppy's eyes. At the same time, the child will very quickly and automatically reach out with their hands to touch the puppy. The puppy will class this as a threat. This is purely down to eye contact between the child and the puppy as in the wild, where puppies and dogs live in packs. When a dog comes into contact with a strange dog that isn't related as part of their pack, they class this outsider as a threat. The two dogs will give visual eye contact towards one another to try and warn off the weaker, less dominant dog. They will start to growl in order to gain dominance over the weakest one and try to take control of being the pack leader. A young pup may see a child in exactly the same way, a threat. As the child gets closer to the young puppy, the child will look directly into the pup's eyes. The puppy classes this as a threat, and will back away and may start to growl, he may also become fearful and aggressive towards the child and try to warn the child off. This reaction is normal. The puppy is doing what he would normally have done in the wild if in a pack with other dogs showing dominance, defending himself and his territory. Some dogs today have more of a stronger pack animal instinct, dominance in them than other breeds of dogs.

Do not let your puppy jump up. Make sure the child does not overexcite the puppy. Try and keep the puppy calm at all times. The moment the puppy starts to get overexcited, pull him away and walk him in the opposite direction. When you're out walking and you come into contact with a child, do not let the puppy pull on the lead. If he does start to pull, give him a gentle tug on the lead and say with a firm tone in your voice 'NO'. If he still persists, walk the pup in the opposite direction away from the child and command the word 'heel'.

Dogs are domesticated by human beings, but still today unbeknown to most people, dogs still use their pack animal instincts. This is inbuilt in them from birth and is survival of the fittest, which could be life or death to them when they were in the wild. There are many reasons if a young dog isn't socialised from a young age why they may bite a child, and the number of warnings from the dog may vary. Just a child walking can be considered a threat to a young dog, even though the child may just want to touch the young dog, and again the dog may growl at the child to warn the child off. Few dogs will actually bite a child without giving some form of warning. Small children don't recognise the warning signs when a dog is growling. The child may still continue to pet or run after the young dog even though the dog is still growling. This is when the dog may bite the child because the dog classes the child as a threat. The dog will instinctively go into fight or flight mode, and again this is a strong animal instinct in the domesticated dog today and is perfectly normal when something strange happens that the dog classes as a threat.

It depends on the size of the threat and how the dog behaves towards it. A nervous and fearful dog will be more threatened than a more stable dog. When someone enters their area of territory, the dog sees this as a threat, he will automatically go into flight or fight mode. He will either run away or defend himself. If he cannot run away, he will fight instead, no matter how afraid he is. This depends on the dog and how fearful he becomes, he may choose to fight first, rather than run away to protect himself.

As mentioned before, dogs do not see children as adults. A child can instantly provoke a dog to bite because children scream, throw their arms about, run, throw things which in turn will trigger off in the dog a predator-prey reaction that is in all dogs today. Some breed of dogs have this instinct more than others and have a stronger inbuilt reaction to other breeds. Another reaction in a dog, sometimes missed by their parents, is when a child plays tug of war. This will result unknowingly to the child rough playing with the dog and will encourage the dog to use its teeth when playing tug of war with the child. The dog will quickly learn this as being acceptable behaviour as though it were in the pack in the wild. The pack animal instinct in dogs is the same when they play together in the litter with their brothers and sisters. They use their teeth and will wrestle and bite one another. This is a form of play training and the start of bringing out the dominant side of the puppy. Just by stroking a dog while he is eating can make a dog growl. If the child carries on stroking the dog, the dog may bite the child. The dog classes the child as a threat because the child has entered into the dog's territory—its safety zone. The dog will then go into fight or flight. If the dog tries to get away or tries to warn the child off with no response, the dog has no alternative but to protect its territory. This is normal, instinctive behaviour in all dogs today. The dog is only responding to what he classes as a threat and is doing what his instincts tell him to do. Remember, dogs do not react or think like people. Looking direct into the dog's eyes can provoke it and make a dog bite. If children are supervised at all times when being introduced to a puppy or a young dog, the dog will eventually learn to trust and except the child and eventually will not associate the child as a threat. Again, it's all part of training the young puppy when socialising to learn, accept and trust different situations and people.

Chapter 7

Transportation

All dogs will have to be transported in a vehicle at some point in their life. You will need to consider what type of carrier the pup will travel in. A young puppy needs to be in a confined space to eliminate injury and any accidents that may happen.

Types of Carriers

There are many types of dog carriers and crates on the market. Almost all pet centres will sell a wide range of transporters and protection for your vehicle. These will include plastic dog carriers which come in various sizes, ranging from the small carriers to very large dog carriers.

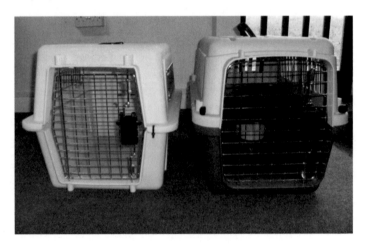

But beware, plastic carriers may look good but can be chewed if the youngster is left for long periods of time on his own. There are also carriers made of material that can be rolled up when not in use and are easily stored away. They come in various sizes and colours. All of these carriers have a fly screen material mesh as well.

The drawbacks of using this type of carrier are if you have to brake suddenly, the puppy will be thrown around in the carrier in the back of the vehicle. This may result in the puppy injuring itself and also the material that the carrier is made of cannot withstand the razor sharp teeth of a puppy going through the teething stage.

Other types of carriers are dog guard/dividers. They come in various sizes to fit different makes of vehicles. They literally separate the dog from getting through to the front of the vehicle while driving. The pup will still have a free run in the back of the vehicle. The disadvantage of using a dog guard/divider is the risk of the youngster being thrown around in the back of the vehicle if you have to apply the brakes suddenly and again could cause injury to the youngster in the process.

One of the other disadvantages: it will not stop the youngster from chewing your vehicle even while being transported, or from throwing up as they do from time to time. A small puppy could wriggle its way through a small gap to lick the back of your head while driving, in an attempt to try and gain your attention.

One of the best carriers now available on the market and one of the most popular are collapsible metal dog cages. They do exactly what they say on the tin. They collapse fully flat when not in use and can be stored away in either the garage or the house or better still can be left flat in the back of the vehicle. The really good thing about using these types of carriers is that they can't be chewed; most of them have a removable tray in the bottom as well.

If in the event your youngster suddenly throws up or has an accident, the tray can quickly be taken out and wiped down clean. Another good reason why I recommend these carriers is that the youngster is completely confined and can be left for short periods on its own, without the fear of coming back to your vehicle to find the back seats half eaten away. It will stop the youngster from shaking the excess mud and water off after a walk as well. Again, if you have to apply the brakes suddenly, the youngster is in a confined space, which limits the amount of area the youngster will slide around and hence reduce any injuries occurring.

If you use a boot liner in conjunction with the metal dog cage, just in case accidents happen, the boot liner will protect the floor of your vehicle and is easily wiped clean as well.

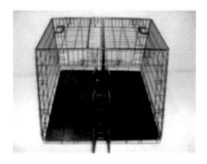

The size of the carrier is important. You don't want a massive carrier to start off with. You will want a carrier that has a big enough space for the youngster to sit or lay comfortably and have enough space to move around in. This way, it will feel more secure. Whatever you buy, make sure the door opens outwards at the front of the carrier. I would recommend you purchase a carrier taking into consideration that the youngster will grow into an adult dog. By purchasing a larger carrier, the youngster will also have the benefit of spending the early days in the carrier especially when you bring the puppy home from the breeder. One half of the carrier can be used as the sleeping area, the other for the youngster's initial toilet area. So, the size of the cage needs to be a bit bigger to take these things into consideration and it will be money well spent.

Introduction to the Vehicle

The very first experience your puppy had in a vehicle was the journey home. This in itself was a traumatic experience for it. The pup will remember being taken away from its mother, brothers and sisters and the warm safe place of the security of its pack. The youngster has never been alone before, let alone been in a car. The second experience it will have in a vehicle will be going to the vets for its vaccinations and being handled by a strange person. This will be yet another traumatic experience for the young pup. Never tie the pup to the inside of the carrier. It's better to leave it loose in the carrier. The young puppy will settle much better when left to its own devices. Introduction to the vehicle can be a long process depending on how the youngster reacts to it, and this may take several weeks or months and a lot of patience is needed to get the pup fully accustomed to travelling.

For the first few days and before taking the pup on a short journey, in order for the pup to get accustomed to the vehicle, put the carrier in the back of the vehicle, when it's feeding time, put the pup in the carrier and make a fuss of the youngster. This will help to regain its confidence back. Once the pup is calm, feed the pup in the carrier. The pup will then start to associate going in the carrier in the back of the vehicle with something nice, which is food. Don't forget the last time the youngster was in the back of the vehicle, it went through a traumatic experience which was being parted from its mother, brothers and sisters, so you will need to build the youngster's confidence gradually again over a period of time.

Again, when it's feeding time, feed the pup in the carrier in the back of the vehicle and continue this over the next week or so until his confidence grows. The pup will usually show signs of excitement when he starts running to the vehicle because he knows he will be fed. The next stage is building the youngster's confidence further and as before, put the pup in his carrier and feed him. While he is eating, start the engine, make a fuss of the youngster reassuring him there is nothing to be afraid of. Do not at this point drive or move the vehicle, let the engine tick over. Over the next couple of weeks, carry on feeding him in the carrier while the engine is running. He will soon get used to the sound of the engine and again associate this with something nice, which is food. After another week if all has gone well, put the pup in the carrier but do not feed him.

As before, start the engine of the vehicle. Give your puppy a biscuit and his favourite toy to take his mind off the noise of the engine running. He will eventually associate being in the carrier in the vehicle with something nice—a biscuit and his toy. Quietly drive the vehicle very slowly just down the road and back. This needs to be a very short journey. Once you get back, make a fuss of the youngster and feed him in the vehicle immediately. If this is done over the next couple of weeks, he will soon get used to the vehicle and the short travels and again will associate this with something nice, which is food.

Once the youngster is settled and shows no signs of stress with the short distances, the next step will be to drive a short distance where you can stop, take the pup to a grassed area so he can stretch his legs and play. Again, he will gradually associate the vehicle with something nice, going to a grassed area to play. Afterwards, put the pup back in his carrier in the vehicle, slowly drive home and feed him as usual in the carrier. If there is no grassed area available where you can let him stretch his legs, bring him back home, put him in the garden and play with him for a short while and then feed him.

A word of warning, make sure before you take the pup out in the vehicle, he has not been fed for at least two hours prior to travelling. This will help eliminate the possibility of him being sick. My experience of puppies being sick is going around corners too quickly, driving too fast and applying the brakes suddenly. Like children, pups and even adult dogs can suffer from motion sickness and together with this, they become stressed as well. Making the journey just a short drive down the road and back slowly will help reduce the youngster's stress levels. Drive with extreme care and try and make the journey as smooth and comfortable as possible. If the pup shows no signs of anxiety or stress, the distance can be extended a bit further over the next couple of weeks. Always try and reward the pup with something nice at the end of each journey. If the pup starts to show any signs of anxiety, i.e. panting, pacing, howling, barking etc., go back to the beginning feeding the pup in the vehicle with the engine running only. Continue to do this process repeatedly until the youngster feels fully comfortable with no signs of stress. The process of getting the pup used to a vehicle can either take a matter of a few days or months.

Today I have a six-year-old springer spaniel who still does not travel well in the back of a vehicle. This is purely down to stress. If I travel anywhere, I feed her well in advance. I make the trips short, stopping and lifting her out at intervals. I put her stress and anxiety down to the fact that when she was a small pup, she was backwards and forwards to the vets. Over the years, she associated the vehicle with stress and anxiety. Older and even younger dogs with the same problem, I have managed to conquer their stress and anxiety levels and sickness just by taking them on a very short journey in the vehicle. This could be a couple of minutes down the road to a small river where they could play. They soon picked up on this, somewhere nice, going for a drive in the vehicle and then playing in the water. Eventually, they couldn't wait to get in the vehicle because they knew they were going somewhere nice. I would take them to the same place every time this made them remember more easily. It also made them confident and comfortable and their stress levels diminished. If at any time the youngster does show signs of extreme stress, you can cover the carrier with a large cloth. This will usually settle the youngster, lowering its stress levels while being transported.

If you persevere and make the trips short and sweet, stick to the same route, you will crack the transportation and travelling in no time.

Motion Sickness

Dealing with motion sickness in a youngster or an adult dog can be extremely hard to tackle. It can make even the shortest trips extremely stressful not only for the youngster but for the owner as well. Even the boldest of youngsters and adult dogs, motion sickness will put them off from even going near a vehicle. They will associate the motion sickness with something bad which was travelling in the vehicle, feeling unwell and being sick.

What Causes Dog Motion Sickness?

Dog motion sickness is more commonly seen in puppies and young dogs rather than in older dogs, but older dogs can suffer from motion sickness as well, just as travel sickness can affect young children and even adults. One of the main reasons why motion sickness occurs in a puppy is down to the fact that the inner ear structure has not fully formed and developed. When travelling, the pressure starts to build up within the inner ear, making the youngster feel off balance, which causes the sickness. Hence to say, not all dogs will outgrow travel sickness, though many will with time and plenty of patience.

Therefore, in the early days when travelling the youngster in a vehicle, if it has encountered a nasty experience, the youngster will associate travelling with something bad, anxiety and vomiting. Even after the inner ears have fully developed, the youngster will still associate travelling with something bad. Stress plays a big factor as well and can also add to travel sickness. So if your youngster has only ever travelled in the vehicle to go to the vets, he may associate this with something bad.

Signs of Dog Motion Sickness and Stress

Motion sickness in a puppy or even an adult dog can be distressing. There are certain signs you will be able to identify, and these are as follows:

- Excessive drooling and foaming from the mouth
- Constant yawning and making noises whilst yawning
- Whining
- Vomiting
- Lip licking
- Uneasiness
- Listlessness
- Lip smacking
- Difficulties in standing up being off balance
- Falling over

Motion Sickness: Tips for Better Traveling

1. Make the journey as comfortable as possible for the youngster to prevent it from being sick.
2. Don't travel too far. Keep the journey to a minimum until the youngster gets used to being transported.
3. Try and face the dog forward in the vehicle if possible.
4. Talk to the youngster. This will keep its attention on you and reduce the stress levels.
5. Reduce the pressure build up inside the vehicle by lowering the vehicle window a couple of inches while the puppy is travelling.
6. Keep the car well ventilated and cool. Put the air conditioning on when it is a hot day. A hot car will contribute to an unpleasant sensation for your puppy, which will make matters only worse.
7. Reduce the puppy's food intake prior to travelling.
8. Take very short trips to a place your puppy enjoys; this could be to a place where the pup can play with

other dogs or a favourite walk, taking your puppy to the same familiar place, he will associate the travel with something nice at the end. This will slowly build his confidence and he will be able to gain tolerance for longer trips.

9. Buying special toys to keep him occupied when he is in the vehicle.

10. Get the puppy used to sitting in the vehicle with the engine turned off. Give him a biscuit as a reward. Once he is confident, turn the engine on and let the engine run while your puppy is in the vehicle.

11. Spend time with your puppy, don't leave him alone in the vehicle for long periods of time.

Motion Sickness Medications

There are various medication on the market that can be purchased at most pet stores specifically for motion sickness and stress, and also your local veterinary can help in reducing the sickness and stress levels in your puppy by way of a prescription.

Puppies that don't outgrow motion sickness and don't respond to any other alternative traveling techniques over the counter medication can be purchased, which your puppy may benefit from. If these don't work, you may have to seek advice from your veterinary surgeon who will prescribe medication. There are different types of medication specific to motion sickness and stress. These may include:

Anti-nausea drugs

Antihistamines, which can reduce the youngster's motion sickness, reduce drooling, reduce vomiting and provide mild sedation while travelling.

While buying over the counter at your local pet store, be sure to consult with your vet before purchasing any treatment for dogs and puppies with motion sickness. You will need to know the correct dose to give before travelling and also the after-effects it may have.

Motion Sickness Remedies

Like everything, a youngster or even an adult dog will associate what has happened and where it was at the time and will associate the experience with something good or bad. If something bad has happened, it will be difficult to cure and only time, reassurance and plenty of patience is needed to overcome the youngster's fear. If the experience has been a bad one, you will need to replace the fear i.e. motion sickness, with something nice and to eradicate as much as possible the cause of the problem. Even the worst youngster and adult dogs that suffered from acute motion sickness and stress levels have been cured after changing where they are placed in the vehicle when travelling. Don't forget, motion sickness is caused by pressure building up in the inner ear. Just by putting some thought in where you have the pup sitting in the vehicle and reassurance can reduce the pressure building up. When a young puppy or even an adult dog is travelling, the pressure will automatically build up in the vehicle, and this will happen more in the back of the vehicle than the front. Sometimes it's better to start off travelling the youngster in the front of the vehicle, making slow, gradual progress step by step and then gradually getting the pup travelling in the back of the vehicle. By doing this, he will cope much better with the build-up of pressure in his ears because you have taken time to reassure the pup, making a bad situation into a good positive one.

A Tried and Tested Method

I have used this method in the past and found it to be a success, but I also use this today on puppies and adult dogs even in the most severe cases.

1. Firstly, make sure you have a passenger to help for the first few travelling trips to hand.
2. In the passenger's footwell at the front of the vehicle, make sure there is plenty of newspaper on the floor of the vehicle in case the pup throws up.

3. Get your passenger to sit in the front passenger seat with their feet and legs apart.
4. Take the youngster from the back of the vehicle out of the carrier he would normally travel in.
5. Place the youngster carefully on the paper on the floor in between the feet and legs of your passenger.

6. Get your passenger to give the youngster plenty of gently fuss but not too much as this will only overexcite him. Most youngsters and adult dogs like a gentle tickle under their chin or being stroked on their head. Get your passenger to keep reassuring the youngster at all times.
7. Once the youngster is settled, start the vehicle engine. Make sure your passenger is still reassuring the youngster. What we are trying to achieve is to distract the youngster from fear and replace it with something nice, which is plenty of fuss and reassurance from your passenger.

Keep the vehicle stationary and leave the engine running only. If the youngster shows signs of stress, give him a biscuit, but don't overfeed him. This is just to reassure him only and to associate the vehicle with something nice. Keep repeating this over the next few days until the youngster's stress levels have gone.

8. In the next stage, as before, place the youngster in the footwell at the front of the vehicle between your passenger's feet. Get your passenger ready to reassure and talk to the youngster as before. Start the engine, take a short, slow trip down the road and back. Get your passenger to reassure the pup by gently talking to the youngster at all times. If this is repeated over the next couple of weeks, you should find that the youngster will quickly associate when he's in the vehicle with something nice. Once this has been achieved, you may find that the youngster may start to get in the front passenger footwell on his own and starts to look forward to travelling longer distances with no signs of sickness and stress. You can then move onto the next stage.

9. Get your passenger to sit in the back seat of the vehicle. Place the youngster on the newspaper in the footwell between the passenger's feet and legs.

10. Travel a short distance down the road and back. Get your passenger to give the pup a biscuit to take his mind off traveling. Make sure your passenger gives the youngster plenty of gentle fuss and talks to him at all times. Over a period of time repeat these short trips, once he is fully confident and wants to get in the vehicle on his own showing no signs of fear or anxiety, the next stage will be travelling him in the carrier in the back area of the vehicle.

11. Put the carrier in the back of the vehicle with some newspaper in it, get your passenger to sit in the back seat as before, put the youngster in the carrier where your passenger can lean across and reassure the pup. Travel a short distance down the road and back. Get your passenger to give the pup a biscuit and plenty of fuss talking to him at all times, this will help distract the youngster. Over a period of time keeping the trips short, you can take the youngster to a favourite place to play or visit a friend who has a dog that your youngster can play with. The aim is for the youngster to associate the travel with something nice. Keep the trips short, once he is fully confident and wants to get in the vehicle on his own, showing no signs of fear or anxiety, you can then progress onto longer trips.

This technique has proven a success over the years, but all dogs and youngsters differ in the time it takes getting them accustomed to travelling without fear and anxiety, depending on how severe the motion sickness is. For some dogs, it may take just a couple of weeks; however, with other dogs, it may take months, but most of them will outgrow it given time once their confidence grows. Once this has been achieved, you will be able to transport the youngster in a carrier in the back of the vehicle on his own without the need of a passenger.

Chapter 8

Basic Training When to Start

I am often asked when should I start training a puppy and how old should the puppy be. I am a firm believer that all puppies are different in their ability and their nature. It also depends on whether the puppy is of a strong nature or soft-natured type. Some pups need the start of basic training at about six months of age. In reality, from the onset of bringing the pup home and unbeknown to the owner, training has already begun. On a general point, all puppies are very different from one another, training is all down to how you bring out the best to your advantage in training the youngster.

As the pup gets older, you will find that he has started to get more independent, adventurous and more inquisitive. You may also notice the pup starts to ignore you at times and is more interested in something else that has captured his attention. He may become more interested in his surroundings; he may become bored and it may be increasingly difficult to hold his interest. Over the weeks, you may find that the youngster will be more in control of you and not you in control of the youngster. This is purely down to the fact that he is now trying to be the dominant leader of the pack, and this would naturally happen with all dogs in the wild. You will have to be patient and firm throughout and show him that you are the pack leader by being persistent with the youngster in gaining his attention in a firm but gentle manner.

There is nothing worse than seeing a boisterous disobedient youngster that doesn't do as he is told. He seems to be taking the owner for a walk, pulling on the lead, barking at everything that moves. This is all because he is trying to show dominance as pack leader. On the other hand, it's so nice to see a well-behaved youngster that walks to heel, sits when told to and quietly takes praise when he has done well. The biggest praise of all goes to the owner who has taken the time and patience to train the youngster. In turn, the youngster shows trust, loyalty and affection to his master.

Play Training Basics

Play training and the basics can start as early as six to eight weeks of age. By twelve weeks of age, your puppy can easily learn basic commands simply by teaching him how to learn and respond while play training. Puppies that enjoy play training eagerly understand commands from you as they mature and grow and can be taught a lot of things when you are play training with them. Their minds are like a small sponge, the puppy will absorb lessons easily and very quickly, forming a strong bond with their owner as they develop and grow.

The puppy at a very tender age learns to trust you in what you are telling it to do. If play training or part of the training goes wrong, this can have a massive impact on the youngster from the onset of his training and years ahead.

One of the first commands you will teach the youngster is calling him by his name. As the puppy starts to get inquisitive and more adventurous, you will find that you need to exercise more control over him for the pup to recognise you are the pack leader. Observing the puppy will give you an indication when to start the basics of training. Starting with the play training stage, this will lay the foundations going forward for the next stage of training.

The Recall

Basic training can start even in the early weeks of getting a new puppy home after the initial settling-down period in its new home. It's important to do things at the same time each day, getting the young puppy into a good routine. Training at feed times can be another way of basic training, and this will get the puppy familiar with being called by his name.

1. At feeding times, have a helper hold the puppy gently a few feet away from you.
2. Put his dish of food on the floor a little distance away from him.
3. Call the puppy by his name and gently clap your hands, at the same time get your helper to release the puppy.
4. Again, call the puppy by his name and gently clap your hands.
5. The puppy will run to his dish for his feed. Give him some fuss while he is eating. If this is done every time he is fed, he will soon get used to his name being called and associate being called with something nice, which is his food.

There are three things your puppy will learn over a period of time:

1. He will learn his name.
2. He will come to you when called.
3. He will learn to be touched while eating.

Some puppies and dogs show signs of aggression while eating. This could be just a growl or snapping. If he growls or snaps at you, this is purely down to the pack animal instinct in him, which is the survival of the strongest. He will eat his food as though it is his last; again, in the wild, dogs would do just that. If another dog enters into his safety area, he would class the intruder as a threat and would either warn him off or fight. In reality, the pup classes you as the intruder and not the pack leader. Touching your puppy every time he is fed will make him soon associate you as his pack leader and not a threat.

Another way of teaching your puppy to come to you can be achieved by calling his name and clapping your hands.

Once you get his attention, put a doggy biscuit on the floor where he can see it. Over a period of time, he will learn when you call his name, he will associate coming to you with something nice—a treat. This can be done either inside the house or outside in the garden, which he is familiar with.

Calling your puppy to come to you

Stronger-natured puppies will always try to be dominant over their owner. A puppy will sense your confidence and how you feel and will quickly pick up on this. At the same time, he will try and take control. If he thinks you are weaker than him, he will try and be the pack leader. If this happens, your puppy may become unruly and naughty. This may result in excessive barking, yapping jumping up for no apparent reason, trying to get your attention. He may start chewing items, pulling on the lead, barking at mealtimes running backwards and forwards. You must always remain the dominant leader of the pack at all times over the puppy. This is very important, but also remain calm and firm with him as well.

'No' Command

The 'NO' command is one of the most important command a young puppy can be taught along with tone of voice. You should teach your puppy to respect you as the pack leader at home. A good daily routine, lots of praise and being consistent at all times on a regular basis will help in training your puppy, setting the foundations as to what he is allowed and not allowed to do.

When your puppy picks up an item he is not allowed, in a firm but gentle voice, give the command, 'NO'. If the pup ignores you say the 'NO' command, again, and quietly go up to the puppy, gently taking the item away from him again with the firm command, 'NO'. Over a period of time when he picks something up that he is not allowed, he will soon learn very quickly the command, 'NO' and will then drop it.

'Down' Command

The down command can also be taught when your puppy starts jumping up at you or family members. When the pup jumps up, quickly place your hands on him, gently pushing him down saying, in a firm but gentle voice, the command, 'DOWN'. If this is repeated every time he tries to jump up, he will soon get the message that this sort of behaviour is not allowed. If he jumps up at other family members, they must also quickly place their hands on him, pushing him down gently, repeating the DOWN command. Do not overexcite your puppy as this will only make him jump up more, which will only confuse him.

Fetch Command

If you have a very inquisitive, bright puppy that needs a lot of stimulation, rolling a ball while the puppy is being held, it can easily be taught the command, 'FETCH'.

1. Sit on the floor.
2. Gently hold the puppy.
3. Slowly roll the ball away from him.

4. Immediately release the puppy and at the same time say 'FETCH'.

Let the puppy run after the ball. Again, if you call his name with a bit of luck, he may bring the ball back. But this may take some practice in getting him to bring the ball back to you. Keep practising with your puppy to fetch his ball with the FETCH command, with short play sessions. He will soon learn if he brings the ball back to you, you will throw it again for him and the puppy will associate this with something nice. If he doesn't respond bringing the ball back, have a second ball ready to hand and gently roll this in front of him to gain his attention commanding him to FETCH, he will more likely drop the first ball and run after the second ball. When he comes back with the ball, reward him with a treat. Over time, he will associate bringing the ball back with something nice, a treat and some fuss.

When Training Goes Wrong

Undoubtedly, if the basics of any training goes wrong, it can have a dramatic effect on how the young dog behaves later on in life. As an example, I was asked to help try to resolve a problem in a young dog that would not come back to its owner when the dog was called. The youngster would come to the recall command but would stop and stay at a distance, neither would the dog let the owner get near or put the slip lead over the dog's head. The young dog would just run away when approached. After a lot of observation not just with the youngster but also on how the owner handled the dog, I soon realised it was down to the owner in the early days when the dog was just a few weeks old. The owner would call the puppy. When the puppy approached the owner, the owner would reach out very quickly and grab the puppy in an attempt to try and get the slip lead quickly over the puppy's head, thus causing the problem later on the pup not wanting to return to its owner. In the pup's head, the last thing the pup remembered was not being called by the owner but being grabbed by the scruff of the neck and having the slip lead pulled over its head. The next time the pup was called, the pup would only return halfway and remained at a distance purely because of fear. In the youngster's mind it associated coming back to the owner with something bad, being grabbed by the neck, which made the youngster fearful in returning.

Just slight, rough handling by the owner can have a huge impact in the early days of training. All training from the onset must be given with a clear, calm voice. The puppy must associate the training sessions with something nice. The pup will then learn to trust and see you as the pack leader in what you are telling the pup to do.

Observations: What Went Wrong

After a lot of observation not only of the youngster but also observing how the owner communicated and handled the young dog, the problem was easily resolved. It was clear that the youngster was afraid of being grabbed and having a slip lead pulled over its head. Unbeknown to the owner, when the owner grabbed the youngster, the owner looked directly into the youngster's eyes. In the wild, when a dog confronts another dog, they would have direct eye contact with each other and would class each other as a threat and would retaliate either with fight or flight. The fight would show dominance in the stronger of the dogs as the pack leader, the weaker one would flight (run away).

How This Was Resolved?

To rectify the situation, it took time and plenty of patience in gaining the youngster's confidence. I used a separate collar and lead instead of a slip lead.

After a few days wearing a collar, I called the youngster in the same way as before. When the youngster started to get close, I literally turned my back and walked away. This made the youngster think he was being left behind. I made no attempt at this point to put the youngster on a lead.

I repeated the same steps over the next few days. It quickly became obvious the youngster was worried about being left behind. The youngster then started to slowly follow me when I walked away.

When in the wild if a young dog is left behind by his pack, their natural reactions would be to follow the pack. If not, he would be vulnerable to predators left on his own, without the security in numbers, so he will stay close to the pack at all times for protection.

Around a week later, I took a biscuit and held it in my hand. I called the youngster by its name. As the youngster started to get close, I turned my back, but this time, I did not walk away, I stood still on the spot. As the youngster came closer, still with my back to him and with no eye contact from me at all, he began to sniff the biscuit I was holding. I then let him take the biscuit from my fingers.

The youngster soon learnt that being called by his name and coming back to me associated this with something nice, which was the reward—a biscuit.

After a couple of weeks, I called the youngster by his name. As he started to get closer, I did not turn my back but quietly knelt down to the youngster's level, at the same time giving him no eye contact at all. I then gave him a biscuit. After a few more days doing this, the youngster would confidently return to the recall for a biscuit and some fuss.

At no stage did I try and clip the lead onto the youngster's collar or give any eye contact. The idea was to gain his confidence and not to frighten or intimidate him in anyway.

A further week doing exactly the same routine worked its magic. Unbeknown to the youngster, when he was recalled, he associated being called with something nice—a biscuit.

Once the youngster's confidence had grown in coming back to me, I was then able to give eye contact without him classing me as a threat. At this point, I was then able to gently clip the lead onto his collar without the youngster knowing, at the same time giving him some fuss. The problem was then resolved. The youngster's fear of being frightened had disappeared. He did not class me as a threat but classed me as the pack leader who he could trust. It is so very easy in the early days to frighten a young dog, which will have an impact on the dogs training later on down the line.

Dogs and human beings play a similar part to dogs in the wild. Human beings have to show they are the dominant pack leader over the dog. The dog has to do what he is told to do and not the other way around. As with all dogs, even though they are domesticated, they still have a strong animal instinct in them. In particular, certain breeds of dogs may have a stronger pack leader instinct in them, more than other breeds. Human beings should take the role of being the dominant leader of the pack. The youngster will then associate you as being in control.

Chapter 9

Training Begins

The very basics of training for a youngster are the foundations set for further advanced training. If the basics are instilled correctly in the youngster, it will be far easier to give more advanced training later on. There are thirteen points to training which include:

- Recall command
- Recall using a long lead
- Recall using a whistle
- The three in one command: SIT, STOP, STAY
- Treat reward training
- Treat reward Sit Command
- Sit command using voice
- Sit command using voice and hand signal

Key Points to Remember

- Lead training how and when to begin
- Lead Training Sit command
- Lead training Heel work
- Traffic Work Lead Training Commands
- Heel Command
- Sit Command

Each stage of training has two key factors to it. For example, you will call the pup by his name, he will come to you and you will reward him with something nice. This will either be a gentle stroke or a dog biscuit. In turn, this will stimulate the youngster to trust you and associate you with something nice.

1. The first key factor will be calling the pup by his name.
2. The second key factor will be praising the youngster when he comes to you.

The biggest key in training a youngster I have found over the years is that your puppy has to build up such a bond and trust in you that when you are giving him a command, the puppy or older dog has to trust you in what you are telling him to do.

Recall Command

The recall is simple. The pup is being called by his name; he instantly should come to you. Keep the lessons very short, five or ten minutes at a time and no more. Remember to leave on a good note. If the pup shows he is getting bored, quit the lesson. Do not keep going over and over the same lesson; keep the lessons short. Never raise your voice at the pup, always keep a soft tone.

Take the puppy into the garden. Make sure you have a few doggy biscuits in your pocket as a just in case. Let the puppy scamper about. Kneel down to the pup's level and call him by his name; clap your hands at the same time. This will distract him from what he is doing. Again, if he doesn't come to you, call him by his name and clap your hands. If he is reluctant, have a biscuit in your fingers ready so he can see it. When he comes to you, make a big fuss of him and give him the treat. If he is still reluctant, don't reach out and grab him, this will only make him feel intimidated. Let him come to you, make it a game. If he is still very reluctant to come when called, stand up, call his name again, clap your hands and walk away from him. A youngster will normally worry he is being left behind and will start running after you. When he comes to you, get down on your knees and make it a game and then give him a treat. Don't try and catch him, this will only frighten him. Just reward him and make a fuss of him, he will soon learn very quickly. As he grows older, you won't need to get down to his level but stand normal. The technique of getting down to a pup's level is to make the pup feel less intimidated by your height. Practice these five or six times a day. Keep the lessons short. Do not bore the youngster.

Recall command using a long lead

Another technique I use on a reluctant pup is an extendable lead. The lead is sprung-loaded and unwinds and rewinds itself on a plastic role, and there is no dangling lead for the pup to get its legs caught up in. The lead itself extends as the pup goes out further and retracts as the pup comes closer to you. Long leads can be purchased at any good pet store in various sizes.

Extendable lead

1. Clip the extendable lead onto the pup's collar. Make sure you have a biscuit ready in your hand.
2. Roll a small ball or gently throw his favourite toy just a few feet away from him. The pup will automatically run after it; in the same way, get down on your knees to the pup's level, clap your hand and call him. If he ignores you, call him again, clap your hands and gently reel him in on the lead. Entice him with the biscuit. When he comes to you, give him the biscuit, make a fuss of him.

After half a dozen times of doing this, the pup will quickly connect the recall and the biscuit with something nice.

Once the pup thoroughly understands and starts to come to you instantly, you can then practice this off the lead in the same way in the garden, which the pup is familiar with. When he has learnt the recall command coming back to you, reward him every now and then so he doesn't always expect a reward, and replace it with some fuss. Remember to keep the lessons short and sweet. If you overdo the training sessions you will start to bore the youngster, and his concentration will drop, he will start to become naughty. The aim is to leave your training sessions on a good note.

It's all about repeating the same thing over and over again. If when you're training, you think the training isn't working, do not try and do something different. You will only confuse the youngster, as he clearly will not understand. This, in turn, will make training longer and will cause problems later on as he grows.

Recall Using a Whistle

Most pet suppliers will sell a variety of whistles and these vary from the silent whistle that only dogs can hear and whistles with a pitch tone in them that humans can hear as well.

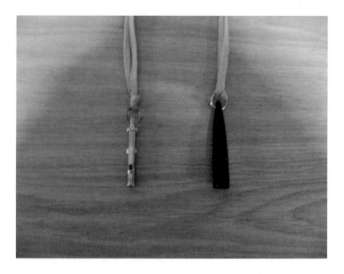

Types of Whistles

Teaching the youngster to come to you can be achieved by using a whistle, but he will have to understand the recall by voice before training to come back to you using the whistle. I have found using a whistle very effective in training working dogs and can be used on puppies as little as five months old. Do not move onto the next step of training until the puppy thoroughly understands the recall and whistle command. The puppy will soon learn the call of his name and the short pips on the whistle. He will associate this with something nice, which will be a reward. Once he understands the recall and the whistle, you can start to recall him when he is playing with his toys. Again, have a treat ready.

1. Clip the extendable lead onto the puppy's collar, stand three or four feet away from him while the pup is occupied scampering about playing with his toys. Get down to his level, call his name and give two short pips on the whistle. Once you gain his attention and as he comes to you, give him a treat.

2. If he is reluctant, roll a ball in front of him. Let him go after the ball. Again call his name, give two short pips on the whistle, and at the same time gently pull him in on the lead. As he gets close to you, give him a treat.

    Doing this over and over again, he will associate the recall and the whistle with something nice. Once he learns and starts immediately responding to you, you can start to extend the lead further but still keep him in an enclosed area of the garden.

3. It's important at this stage you make sure you stay close to the pup when recalling him. This is all part of the basic training process and lays the foundation to extend this as the pup gets older. It's all about reward training and associating the training with something nice.

    When the pup thoroughly understands the recall, you can then take him to an unfamiliar place, i.e. a friend's garden or an open field or park. If he has been taught the training correctly, he should respond in the same way as before, but beware, if you take him to a new place, there will be more distractions, and he may become more inquisitive.

4. Clip the extendable lead onto the pup's collar. Gently let him play; roll a ball or throw his favourite toy to distract him. As before, call his name, get down to his level and give two short pips on the whistle. Once he comes to you, give him a treat. If he's reluctant, give a gentle tug on the lead, once he gets close to you, give him a treat as a reward.

The Three in One Command – SIT, STOP, STAY

The three in one command, I like to call this the 'SIT, STOP, STAY' command because that is exactly what it is. You tell the youngster to sit; he has also stopped and is also staying put on the spot. In my experience, the sit command is probably the most important command you will ever teach a youngster because it is not only the sit command but also the stay position as well. If you can get a dog to sit and stay routed to the spot while walking away from him without the dog moving, you will be onto a winner in having an obedient and well-trained dog. The bonus will be that you have trained your dog well.

Treat Reward Training

Lure Treat Reward Training is a good way of stimulating your puppy. He will focus more on what you are telling him to do and he will quickly associate this with something nice, which is a treat and some fuss. Not only this, with plenty of patience and repetition you can also teach your puppy all kinds of new things using treat rewards.

There are several types of training techniques today, but the tried and tested is treat training which uses a treat reward to lure the youngster into the sit position gently. Lure Treat

Reward Training can be another way to teach your puppy to sit. It is easy and fun not just for your puppy but for you as well. The Treat Reward can also be taught on adult dogs as well. They can learn quite quickly with this type of training. This type of training involves using a dog biscuit to guide a puppy or dog into the position where you want him to be. Most puppies and dogs are motivated by food, but if he is not you can use his favourite toy instead.

Treat Reward Sit Command

1. Stand directly in front of your puppy and tell him to SIT. Speak to your puppy in a firm, but gentle, voice; do not shout at him. At the same time hold the treat just above the puppy's nose just a few centimetres away so he can smell it but not eat it; again, tell him to SIT.

Slowly lift the treat upward and over the top of your puppy's head, making sure you do this slowly. The aim is to get your puppy's nose to follow the treat upwards and over his head.

The pup should follow the treat with his nose, and at the same time, his rear end will sit on the ground. As soon as his rear end touches the ground, tell him to SIT, give him the treat and praise him.

If you find your puppy backing away or jumping up, it is because you are holding the treat too far away from him or you are moving the treat to quickly up and over his head. You will have to hold the treat close to the puppy's nose in order for the puppy to be able to smell the treat in your figures. Slowly in your fingers, take the treat up and over his head, repeat these steps until the puppy responds to you, telling him to SIT once his bottom touches the ground. Practice this over and over again for five or ten minutes, just short sessions every day until he understands what you are asking him to do. Again, each time he sits, reward him, he will soon learn. If he sits when you tell him to, he will associate this with something nice, either with praise or a treat. Make sure he fully understands the SIT command before you move onto the next training session.

Sit Command Using Voice

2. Put your puppy on a lead and stand next to him. The lead will have to remain fairly tight; at the same time, gently press down on your puppy's rear end and command him to SIT. As soon as your puppy is in the sitting position, give him a treat and some fuss. Keep repeating this every day, especially at mealtimes. He will soon associate the sit command with something nice—food and some fuss.

Push the puppy's bottom down to sit

Once he responds to the word SIT, you won't need to press on his bottom or have him on a lead. He will just sit when you tell him to and again he will associate this with something nice. For some puppies, it may take longer, as with all puppies, some learn quicker than other puppies, and you will have to be patient until he thoroughly understands what is required of him. Meal time is a good starting point in teaching the puppy to sit.

Sit Command Using Voice and Hand Signal

3. Once the puppy understands what the SIT command means, from just your voice, you can now bring in the SIT command with a hand signal. Put the lead on your puppy and stand next to him. Again, keeping the lead fairy tight, place the flat palm of your hand directly in front of your puppy just above his head; at the same

time, tell him to SIT. The puppy should sit. By using the word SIT together with the hand signal each time, the puppy will begin to associate the hand signal with the SIT command and should put the two together. You will need plenty of patience and time in teaching the puppy the SIT command. If he is reluctant, gently push the puppy's bottom down on the ground in order for him to thoroughly understand what is required of him; each time, command him to SIT. Do not move onto the next stage of training until he is obedient with the SIT command.

Your goal is for the puppy to recognise the hand signal and the SIT command. As soon as the puppy sits to your command backed up with the hand signal, he should be rewarded with something nice—a treat.

Using a hand signal with SIT command

Reward him with a treat every single time he has done well. Make sure you always reward your puppy as well during training sessions, so the puppy looks forward to the lessons and associates these lessons with something nice.

Eventually, when he thoroughly understands the SIT and hand signal command, you can praise the puppy instead of giving him a treat. Do this every second or third time initially. This is called intermittent reward; your puppy will associate something nice with being praised instead of a treat.

Key Points to Remember

I always find that a soft-natured puppy is more biddable to train and work with, whereas the strong-natured puppy will be bolder and take longer to train, and the lessons taking longer for the puppy to understand. The stronger-natured pup is quick to learn and quick to forget. Usually, the mistake made here is that when you think the puppy understands what you are asking of him, you then move onto the next stage of training. But actually the pup doesn't understand, thus later the puppy starts to ignore you and becomes naughty. This is why it takes longer for a strong-headed puppy to train. You have to make sure before moving onto the next step of training your puppy must thoroughly understand what is required of him.

1. Take your time; don't rush the training sessions; keep the lessons to just ten minutes, and always leave on a good note.
2. Never raise your voice as this will only frighten the youngster.
3. Make sure the pup understands 100% before you move onto the next lesson of training, and remember, Rome wasn't built in a day.
4. The pup is still a baby just like a child, his concentration is very short. If you find you have had a bad day and you're irritable, leave the training as the young pup will pick up on how you feel. You can

140

bet if you're in a bad mood, the youngster will not do as it's told and will be naughty.

5. The biggest rule in any training: if the pup has done well, praise it, make a fuss of the pup.

Lead Training How and When to Begin

Most owners find this part of training a difficult task. Time and time again, I have seen young puppies being dragged in all directions behind their owners saying it will learn eventually. Walking on the lead should be a happy experience for your puppy and not a bad experience. Your puppy should get used to wearing a collar as soon as possible. This could be as early as eight to twelve weeks of age or when you bring your new puppy home. The collar must be a comfortable fit, not too tight and not too loose when you first introduce the lead. This should be done at feed times, so the puppy associates the lead with something nice—his food.

Do not be tempted to take the pup in the garden, or expect to walk your puppy out in a public place. For the first few sessions, introduce your puppy to the lead; attach the lead to the collar and leave it hanging loose with no restriction or tension while the puppy is eating his food. Once he has eaten his meal, remove the lead a little while afterwards, introducing the lead this way he will quickly associate the lead with something nice—his food. Every time the puppy is fed, clip the lead onto his collar so he is fully familiar with the lead.

1. After a few days, clip the lead onto the puppy's collar. After your puppy has finished his meal, follow your puppy around holding the lead very loosely, without any attempt to put tension on the lead or to restrict him in any way what-so-ever.
2. Over the next few days, gradually get your puppy accustomed to having some tension on the end of the lead, but, still, keep the lead fairly loose at this point.
3. After a few more days, you can start to shorten the lead a little at a time, but at no point should you

shorten the lead too much as this will only make the puppy pull on the lead. If you get to the point where the puppy sits down and won't budge or starts to pull against you, do not pull the puppy towards you. This will only make matters worse. The puppy will either stay rooted on the spot in the sit position or you will have a tug of war on your hands with your puppy pulling against you in all directions.

4. If your puppy does sit and refuses to move, one simple thing I do is to try and distract the pup. I will turn the situation into play training by rolling a ball in front of him, extend the lead so it's very loose, get down to the pup's level, on your knees, call his name and roll the ball; usually this does the trick and the pup will come running. I will then reward him with a treat. Practice these sessions over and over again. This sort of distraction usually works, make sure you give your puppy plenty of fuss. After a couple of minutes of play training, with the lead loosely attached, you can close the training session and leave on a good note.

5. Never leave on a bad note as this will be the last thing the puppy will remember which will cause further problems later on when training. When the pup is comfortable with the lead, it can be gradually shortened over a couple of weeks. Patience is a key aspect of puppy training; different puppies learn at different stages. This will depend on breeding and also if the puppy is a strong-natured pup or soft-natured. Be prepared for training to take longer than expected; do not get annoyed or frustrated with your puppy.

6. When training your puppy make sure no distractions are going on around him, especially if you are training outside in the garden or in an unfamiliar place, as this will only distract him. He may also start getting excited if there is a lot going on while being trained.

7. Nip problems such as pulling on the lead or lunging forward straight away, while your puppy is still very young. Allowing your puppy to misbehave and get away with this type of behaviour will end up later with your pup taking control of you, trying to be the pack leader. As he grows older, he will start to show dominance towards you, he will become more of a challenge to work with, so do not allow this type of behaviour to happen. If your puppy begins to pull on the lead or tries to run off, turn around and walk off in the opposite direction, keeping your puppy on the outside of you when you turn. The result will be, your puppy will gently be pulled towards you as you walk away; he will feel he is being left behind and will want to follow you. Be prepared to go over these sessions several times, praising him when he has done well and understands what you are asking him to do.

Lead Training Sit Command

Practising this in the house first where it is reasonably quiet. There will be less distractions for the youngster before progressing in the garden. It is no good trying to train the youngster outside if other dogs are running around or there are kids kicking footballs. You must get the youngster's attention on you, and where it will be quiet. Once the youngster is accustomed to walking close to your side, he can then be taken for short walks outside.

1. With the lead attached to the collar, place the youngster at your side and with lead in your hand, which should be fairly short but not too tight, walk a few paces forward with your puppy.

Stop and tell your puppy to SIT. When he responds to your command, give him a treat. Keep him close to your side at all times. Walk forward again quickly three steps with your puppy and then stop; again tell your puppy to SIT. When he sits, give him a treat. Repeating this again, walk forward quickly with your puppy just a few steps. Do not let your puppy get ahead of you. Stop and tell your puppy to SIT. When he responds to your SIT command, give him a treat so he can associate the SIT command with something positive.

Repeat this over the next couple of weeks at least five minutes training session a day. Do not overdo the sessions and always finish on a good note. Once the puppy is obedient and understands, you can then take him somewhere familiar outside and carry on the training sessions. Remember to keep the lessons to five minutes a day only finishing on a good note, when he has done well praise the youngster.

2. If your youngster is reluctant to sit, as before, walk three steps with him at your side, then stop and command the youngster to SIT at the same time gently pushing his bottom on the ground. When his bottom is in the SIT position, give him a treat at the same time reinforcing the SIT command. Every time he is in the SIT position give him the treat as a reward, he will eventually associate this with something positive.

Lead Training Heel Command

Start in the garden first with your puppy so there are fewer distractions, get him accustomed to walking to 'heel' close to your side. He can then be taken for short walks. Have some puppy treats in your pocket in order to give him a treat when he has done well.

1. Put your puppy on a lead, keep him fairy close to you, walk next to him in the same way when you were teaching him to sit at your side.
2. With your puppy at your side, walk forward and at the same time gently tell him to HEEL. Give him a treat in order for him to want to stay close to your side. He will be able to associate walking close to you with something nice—a treat.
3. If your puppy pulls forward, lure him back with a treat. Keep the treat in your hand to get the puppy's attention. Hold your hand just above his nose while he is walking at your side. Keep the treat close to his nose at all times. If you hold it too far away, it may make him jump up at your hand.
4. Again, walk forward slowly, at the same time command the puppy to HEEL. If he starts to lunge forward or pull on the lead, turn in the opposite direction, walk forward pulling him to you gently and command him to HEEL at the same time. Keep the treat close to you so he can smell the treat in your figures.
5. If he keeps lunging forward, walk away in the opposite direction. This will distract him and he will want to follow you. Again, once he is at your side, stop and then walk forward, keeping him close to you and at the same time command him to HEEL; lure him with a treat. Repeat walking in the opposite direction each time he lunges forward ahead. Correct him by saying HEEL, lure him with the treat and once he is walking at your side, give the pup a treat so he can associate being at your side with a reward.

6. If your puppy sulks and sits on his bottom and refuses to move, lure him with a treat, make it as tempting as possible. Walking forward slowly put the treat close to his nose. Once he follows the treat, command him to HEEL and keep praising him. Do not drag him on the lead or scold him. Get your puppy's attention by tempting him with a treat to walk forward.

Puppy refusing to budge

7. After a few sessions, he will soon respond to the 'HEEL' command and will begin to associate the heel command with something nice—a treat.
8. Every time he is in the heel position and walking at your side, reward him with a treat. This will also teach him to look to you for direction as his pack leader, as he would if he were in a pack with other dogs in the wild. As he progresses and starts to understand what you are asking him to do, you can walk your puppy for a longer period at your side before giving him a treat.
9. Keep practising this over the next couple of weeks until he understands walking to heel at your side. When he is happy to walk at your side and obeys your

command to heel, you can then start to drop the treat reward and give him praise instead. When your puppy is fully confident, you can progress to the next step taking him on a short walk and continue his heel training. When taking him on short walks, use the same route initially he will become familiar with the same surroundings and smell., which will build your puppy's confidence, he will associate going out for a walk with something nice.

Traffic Work Lead Training Commands
Heel Command

Once your puppy is accustomed to a collar and lead and all the basics of training, you can progress his training taking him for short walks where there is traffic. This will build his confidence gradually in getting him used to the noise of passing traffic, meeting people with other dogs and meeting children when taking him for a walk. For a soft-natured puppy that has a more nervous disposition, this may take several weeks in gradually getting him accustomed to the noise of traffic and meeting other people and dogs. The aim is to make sure your pup encounters positive experiences when going out for short walks and be able to associate the walks with something nice. Always make sure when taking your puppy for short walks that you always have puppy treats in your pocket just in case he shows any signs of fear. This way, you can turn a negative experience into a positive experience. If he becomes very nervous about a passing vehicle, give him a treat as the vehicle passes him. He will soon learn to associate the vehicle and the noise with something nice—a treat.

Remember, your puppy is only small and has never encountered new situations. He may feel vulnerable and overwhelmed. Try to make your puppy enjoy his walks and make sure he is not frightened at any point. A young puppy will pick up on your own attitude and feelings to a situation. If you feel nervous about a situation, your puppy will sense this. The puppy in his head will sense two things:

1. His pack leader has become scared.
2. The puppy has become even more frightened because his pack leader, which is you, has become nervous .

Remember, you are his pack leader. If you show any signs of being nervous, or you appear concerned or worried about the puppy's reaction to the traffic passing or a situation, your puppy will pick up on how you feel. It will only make him think, ***My pack leader is frightened; something bad may happen***, which will make your puppy more nervous. You will have to turn a negative into a positive which will enable your puppy to feel confident to a particular situation. This is all part of a puppy learning and growing and understanding how to react to different situations when they arise. If you remain calm at all times and in control of your puppy, your puppy will pick up on how his pack leader feels. Your puppy's reaction will be, ***My pack leader will protect me; nothing will harm me.***

As the pup's confidence grows, take him out for walks where there is more traffic. Everything you do with your puppy should be a positive experience. When taking your puppy on short walks, the puppy should always be protected from any fearful situations. He should never be overwhelmed. Get him accustomed to encountering such situations slowly. Do not rush things. Make sure you have plenty of treats at the ready just in case.

'Sit' Command

Keep taking your puppy for short walks where there is some traffic noise on a daily basis, walking him to heel.

Once he is obedient and responsive and shows no signs of being nervous where there is ongoing traffic, you can then start training him on the lead to the command SIT when traffic passes him. Make sure you have plenty of treats in hand.

1. Put your puppy on a lead. Keep him close to your side, and walk forward a few steps. When a vehicle starts to approach, stop and command your pup to SIT. When your pup sits, reward him.
2. Repeat, keeping your puppy close to your side, walk forward a few steps, stop and command your puppy to SIT when a vehicle approaches. When he is in the sit position, reward him immediately. Practice this for five minutes a day while out walking in traffic with your puppy.

If he is reluctant to sit at your side, you can gently push his bottom down when commanding him to SIT. At the same time, hold a treat near to his nose. Once he is sitting, give him the treat.

Dogs with Disabilities

Not only puppies but all dogs can be trained to a reasonable standard, even dogs with disabilities, but training may take longer depending on how serious the disability is. I have trained both male and female dogs over the years and have had some remarkable shooting dogs that have also been trained for gun dog trials as well. One dog, in particular, was a deaf English Springer Spaniel we took on at eight-months-old from a dog rescue centre. We were his fourth owners in his life, his head was very much screwed up due to the incompetence of being passed from owner to owner and not realising he was stone deaf. As such, he incurred extremely rough treatment through the early months of his life, which included being beaten. The previous owners had no idea he was deaf and just thought he was being difficult and naughty. Neither did they know how to train or handle him because of this huge disability.

These owners went on to abusing him out of frustration, which mentally scarred him. His trust in human beings was smashed to bits because of the fear, when he returned, he would get a beating from his owner. In his head, the last thing he remembered was not running off but being beaten when he returned to his owner. Consequently, he would not come back but stayed at a distance. This went on to having several owners in the first eight months of his life. He was a shattered boy.

When he came to me, I was asked if I could train him so they could find him a new home, but after a lot of observations, I soon realised his hearing had never developed. He was stone deaf. I decided at this point to give him a home for the rest of his life. My other dogs quickly took to him as part of their pack. They sensed he had a disability, and in their heads, they would protect him. Some eighteen months later, after a lot of patience and very careful handling, he started to show signs of being able to trust me without the fear of being punished when he did not return. Trained to hand signals, he went on to be one of the best boys I had ever trained. When walking out along with our other dogs, no one would ever know he was deaf. They were amazed that he could work and behave just as well as our other dogs. His eyes were always focussed on what we were telling him to do. He never took his eyes off of us and trusted us completely. Sadly, in 2016 at the age of fourteen, we had to have our lovely boy put to sleep. He will always be remembered in our hearts as being an incredible little dog that is so sadly missed.

Barney, our beloved deaf boy, trained to hand signals

Barney with his companion Della